MW01115851

DEALING WITH THE
IRS

Strategies to reduce and resolve your IRS tax debts

Mike Ornelas, EA

Copyright © 2019. Mike Ornelas

All rights reserved.

ISBN: 9781691477708

DEDICATION

I dedicate this book to my wife, Amelia. My life became sweeter when you entered it. You're the sugar in my coffee. I've become a better man because of your encouragement, support, and strength. You teach me what it means to demonstrate compassion to those less fortunate. I'm constantly reminded of the saying, "behind every great man is a great woman."

While I don't think myself a great man, I know that I have a great woman. I don't take for granted the blessing you are to me. My one regret is that I didn't marry you sooner. Maybe we'd have those six kids 😊. Although it's cliché, I look forward to the next 50 years of our journey together.

Important Notice

While every effort has been taken to ensure that the information contained herein is accurate as of the time of publication, tax laws and regulations are constantly changing.

This book is designed to provide accurate and authoritative information regarding the subject matter covered, but it is sold with the understanding that the publisher is not engaged in rendering legal or accounting services, and no information contained herein should be construed as legal advice.

If legal advice or other expert assistance is required, the services of a competent professional person should be sought. The publisher does not guarantee or warrant that readers who use the information provided in this publication will achieve results like those discussed.

This book does not constitute the guarantee of a specific result as those individuals mentioned. Although the author is engaged in accounting, tax preparation, and tax representation, he does not claim to produce the same results as those mentioned. Each situation is different. The outcomes are based on facts and circumstances of each individual case.

<u>Incredible FREE Gift Offer!</u>

Visit <u>www.SacramentoTaxResolution.com</u> to get your FREE Tax Debt Consultation, a $495 value.

1. From the home page, enter your info where it says, "Do you owe any IRS or state taxes?"

2. Answer the questions.

Voila! Someone from my office will reach out to you!

"Best description I can think of, is a single word.

trust·wor·thy
/ˈtrəs(t)ˌwərT͟Hē/

adjective
able to be relied on as honest or truthful. Mike tells you what he can do and sets out to do it."-**Tom Kinney**

INTRODUCTION

If you owe money to the IRS, then this book is for you.

Whether you're going to tackle the problem yourself, or just want to have a better understanding of what your professional representative is doing (or, unfortunately, sometimes *not* doing), this book is your guide to understanding the whole process.

Tax resolution is the process of satisfying your tax debt. This involves settling the tax debt for less than you owe or paying in full. You can accomplish this through a few different strategies. We'll cover the most effective strategies for dealing with the IRS in the coming pages.

For now, know that there IS hope for getting the IRS off your back. No, you don't need to flee to some desert island. No, you don't need to end your life. No, you don't need to join a monastery. No, you don't need to keep ignoring the problem. No, it won't just go away. Yes, you do need to actually do something to get results.

This book will provide a roadmap to make sure you're on the right track. Even if you choose to go it alone, which I don't recommend, at least you'll be empowered with the necessary information to ensure you're not getting scammed by a cussing, pushy, telemarketer.

Who am I? I got started in the accounting industry when I was just a wee lad of 8. My mom used to bribe me with candy

11

in exchange for doing bookkeeping. Little did I know, my dear old mom was using me to get her work done!

I've been around for a long time. My dad showed me the ropes of the tax business. But I preferred doing my own thing over doing tax returns.

So, I tried my hand at everything else. Like, bookkeeping, answering phones, client follow up, etc.

Then, I hit the jackpot: marketing. I noticed that there were clients who would come to have their taxes done, only to not return the next year. I asked my dad if he did anything to try to get them to come back as clients. He said, "No." I got their mailing addresses and typed up a quick letter with the headline "Baby Come Back."

Many of them called and continued to be loyal clients for many years. I then stumbled upon an opportunity to take the business to the next level by helping clients with their IRS issues. This is something my dad did a little bit of, but not a whole lot. The business was nearly driven by tax preparation.

As a result, having finally heeded my dad's hundreds of pitches, I took, and passed, the IRS's Enrolled Agent Exam. Doing so allowed me to represent taxpayers before the IRS and negotiate deals to settle their tax bills.

See, the little guy, figuratively speaking, is under- represented. My mission is to rid the world of incorrect tax returns, IRS nightmares, and the like. I do this, so I can one day start a charity that helps end poverty by teaching under-privileged children and at-risk youth how to start businesses.

You're reading this because you, or your "friend," are experiencing IRS troubles. This pain causes you anxiety, sleepless nights and becoming your favorite headache medicine's number one customer. Admit it had everything been going good for you, there's no way you'd be reading this.

Fair enough.

But, since you're here, I'm glad you're here. See, in the book, "The Subtle Art of Not Giving a FUC*," Mark Manson says "Pain is our body's most effective means of spurring action.

Give yourself credit.

You may not have tackled your entire IRS issue. But, come on, at least you did *something*. Don't be so hard on yourself.

Success begins with baby steps.

You're in this mess because life happened: divorce, bankruptcy, foreclosure, death of a loved one, job loss, etc. It's not like you woke up one day and thought, "I think I'll purposely NOT pay the IRS. After all, I enjoy the threat of my wages being garnished, bank account levied, and property taken away and sold to pay my past due taxes.

Nope.

See, if your situation is like the many people I've come across, down deep, you're a pretty decent person. Sometimes, bad things happen to good people. It's unfortunate. Buck up. I'm here to help guide you on the path to freedom from the IRS. At least, freedom from the back taxes you owe them.

What would life be like without struggle? Imagine: you wake up every day and life is exactly as you'd like it- you have all the money you could ever want, have all the friends you could ever want, have all the fame you could ever want and look and feel the way you want, all. The. Time.

Would you be happy?

Most likely not. So, consider this IRS issue you're facing an adventure. Because we all know that the person who's been places and seen things is much more interesting than the homebody who just binge watches "Pretty Little Liars."

Overcoming this IRS issue is a journey. You don't get to your destination overnight.

But that's the beauty of it.

You can look back in a year or two and know that, even though this was a grueling experience, you have some interesting stories to tell because you gritted your teeth, braced yourself, and faced the problem head on.

Choose not to be like the kid who so anticipates Christmas morning that, when he gets there, he feels deflated. Enjoy the journey.

But you may be wondering: do I have to do something about this? Can't I just keep my head buried in the sand? Well, you could. Why would you want to? You could be like those people who refuse to embrace the struggle because it doesn't feel good, but, in the words of Nacho Libre, "Don't you want a little taste of the glory? See what it tastes like!"

Yes, I did just use a Nacho Libre quote.

Wouldn't you rather be that guy who's able to say while others refused to face Goliath because of fear, you gladly rode up and conquered him? You CAN be the giant-killer.

You can overcome this challenge, put it behind you, and move forward to a better life. While I'm no self-help guru, I realize there's benefit in giving a pep talk every now and then. See, there have been times when people have been on the verge of throwing in the towel.

That's when they need someone rooting them on.

In an episode of *The Twilight Zone,* John wakes up and is met by a guy who tells him he can have anything he wants. Where does John go first? The casino. There, he finds that he wins every hand he's dealt and every slot he plays. So, John goes back again the next day. Same thing. He wins every time he places a bet. Then he goes back the next day. And the next. And the next. And the next.

John just keeps right on winning.

Is John happy? Quite the contrary. He tracks down the guy who told him he can have anything he wants. John tells him, "I don't understand. This is not how I imagined heaven would be."

The guy replies, "Who said this was heaven?"

As humans, we're hardwired to need a challenge. The greater the obstacle, the better. But tackling the insurmountable obstacle is where the rubber meets the road. Many are simply not willing to put int the time and effort necessary to see

Goliath fall. So, they wallow through their trouble, hoping to blame their way through.

You know what?

It's no one else's fault. Be honest. You didn't get to where you are because it someone else is to blame. Now, I'll admit, maybe the other person's share of the fault is 90%. But, even so, your 10% still helped get you here.

Relax. No judgement here. I'm simply helping to put things into perspective.

It is true that there are times when a divorce happened, and you're left holding the bag. I get it. But, most often, there's no one else to blame except the person staring back at you in the mirror. This is the one who is to blame.

So, if you've decided to get on, and stay on, the straight and narrow, rejoice! You CAN be helped! If you're simply looking for a magic pill to take all your problems away, I'm sorry. There's no such thing.

On the other hand, it typically requires pain for us to act. You don't act when the first IRS notice arrives.

Nope. You act when you get the IRS notice threatening to seize your paycheck or bank account. That's right. It's when the pain of staying the same is greater than the pain of change that we finally act to change. And this has proved to be true hundreds of times.

Take Steven. Now, things were going good for him. Until they weren't. He calls my office one day asking for advice about what to do about his IRS issue. His girlfriend wanted to marry

16

him. But she told him she wouldn't do so until he handled his IRS problem.

He paid another firm, that's now out of business, around $3,000. Alas, they did nothing to help him. So, suffice it to say, he was a bit skeptical. When I told Steven that he could come down to our office, he was shocked. "Wow! You guys are actually easy to get a hold of," he said.

But he still wasn't convinced about hiring me.

After he applied for jobs and was denied due to his IRS debt, he finally signed up.

I'm glad you picked up this book, whether you paid for it or not. Either way, the information on the following pages may just change your life.

I truly wish you the best in your effort to experience a "less taxing" life! Head over to my website www.MikeOrnelas.com to explore more information about me and my services.

-Mike

Chapter 1:

Overview of The IRS And Your Rights as A Taxpayer

The new mission statement of the softer, gentler IRS: The IRS' mission is to "provide America's taxpayers top quality service by helping them understand and meet their tax responsibilities and by applying the tax law with integrity and fairness to all."

Gone (supposedly) are the days when you called the IRS and got a nasty person on the other end of the line. My recent experience has shown that the folks at the IRS are being trained on customer service skills.

That's good news for us all!

However, be aware that this kinder, gentler IRS only pertains to individual income tax issues. If you're a small business owner whose business owes payroll taxes and triggered the Trust Fund Recovery Penalty, you're out of luck.

See, you just don't want to encounter the folks at the IRS responsible for collecting payroll taxes. You just don't. they've been commissioned to get the money. I spoke with a restaurant owner who told me he talked to an IRS revenue agent who cussed, screamed and called him every word in the book.

So, trust me. It's in your best interest to stay in the good graces of the IRS by staying current with your tax return filings, payroll tax return filings, payroll tax deposits and income tax payments.

Two Most Important Rules

Here's the deal—you must stay current and compliant. My mentor, Jassen Bowman, beats this horse dead. Current and compliant is the name of the game. Current and compliant means that you file all tax returns on or before the due date. This includes income tax returns, payroll tax returns, and any other tax related information filings.

You must also stay current.

So, you'd need to not add anymore tax to the balance you already owe to the IRS. The IRS uses the term "snowball" to describe a taxpayer who continues to accumulate tax debt.

If you're an employee who owes back taxes to the IRS, you need to immediately increase your federal tax withholding with your employer. Contact your human resources representative and ask to fill out a new form W-4.

That's the form that allows you to adjust your withholding. Once that's done, make sure you keep an eye on your paycheck in the future. If you anticipate a bonus or a raise, adjust your withholding again. I know, this can be a real pain in the rear end.

Honestly, would you rather go through the minor inconvenience of keeping tabs on your paycheck or have the IRS breathing down the back of your neck?

Right.

On the other hand, if you're self-employed, you've got to make sure to make estimated tax payments in a timely manner. I recommend paying them monthly, so you don't get sticker shock when you pay them quarterly.

The total you pay in estimated taxes for that respective tax year must equal 90% of the tax for the current tax year or 100% of the tax for the prior tax year, whichever is smaller. You need to pay estimated taxes if you anticipate owing the IRS at least $500. If you're expecting a federal tax refund you don't need to make estimated tax payments.

Use the form 1040-ES worksheet to figure your estimated tax payments for the tax year.

If you're a small business owner and you've fallen behind on payroll tax deposits, make the next payroll tax deposit and file the next payroll tax return by the due date. In other words, get current.

Yes, you're not catching up on the past due payroll taxes and payroll tax returns. But doing this step is one of the IRS's prerequisites for agreeing to settle your past due tax liability.

Compliant means that you're following the directions for cooperating with what the IRS is directing you to do. For example, you're either hiring someone to represent you before them or notifying the IRS of your intentions. It also involves being up-front about your filing status and recordkeeping.

Yes, it seems like a lot to get caught up. But, if you really want to end this IRS nightmare, you're going to need to roll up your sleeves and get to work. Most of my colleagues will tell you that the hardest part of helping people resolve their tax problems is getting the information and documents from the client!

I most certainly agree.

For some reason, taxpayers come to me expecting a miracle. Look, last I checked, there was only one person to ever walk on water. And not even he made everyone happy! I tell clients be up-front with me every step of the process or what you want to see happen won't happen. What will happen is you'll get farther behind and end up worse off.

Your Voice at the IRS

The IRS Taxpayer Advocate Service is a division of the IRS that helps hold the IRS accountable. They're "in" the IRS, not "of" the IRS. They help in times of disaster. For example, your case lands on the desk of the IRS agent from hell. He won't budge. He's closed to all logic. And his supervisor is even worse than he is!

Time to call our friends at the Taxpayer Advocate Service, TAS for short. Now, the TAS is usually a last resort. Appeals is next when I encounter an unfair IRS agent. Although it's nice to know that there's another option in case appeals doesn't grant our request, either.

It's going to take some time for TAS to get back to us because their budget has been cut to the bone. I spoke to a supervisor at the local TAS office who said that they're facing many of their personnel retiring in the middle of helping taxpayers! New TAS Agents take 1 or 2 years to be trained to replace the retiring agents.

Unless Congress chooses to increase the federal allocation to TAS, long response times will be the norm. It's nice to know that there's a government department rooting for a successful resolution to your tax case, though.

Tax Resolution Resource

To request help from the Taxpayer Advocate Service, go to their website:

https://www.irs.gov/taxpayer-advocate

If you've tried to reach the Taxpayer Advocate Service and it's been over a month since you first contacted them, be patient. Remember: they're dealing with an unending stream of new cases with limited staff to work those cases. Contact me at Mike@SacramentoTaxResolution.com to request a FREE Tax Debt Consultation. I guarantee we'll reach a resolution!

Your Rights as A Taxpayer

You have many rights as a U.S. taxpayer that you may not be aware of. According to the Taxpayer Bill of Rights:

Taxpayers have the right to know what they need to do to comply with the tax laws. They are entitled to clear explanations of the laws and IRS procedures in all tax forms, instructions, publications, notices, and correspondence. They have the right to be informed of IRS decisions about their tax accounts and to receive clear explanations of the outcomes.

The Right to Quality Service

Taxpayers have the right to receive prompt, courteous, and professional assistance in their dealings with the IRS, to be spoken to in a way they can easily understand, to receive clear and easily understandable communications from the IRS, and to speak to a supervisor about inadequate service.

The Right to Pay No More than the Correct Amount of Tax

Taxpayers have the right to pay only the amount of tax legally due, including interest and penalties, and to have the IRS apply all tax payments properly.

The Right to Challenge the IRS's Position and Be Heard

Taxpayers have the right to raise objections and provide additional documentation in response to formal IRS actions or proposed actions, to expect that the IRS will consider their timely objections and documentation promptly and fairly, and to receive a response if the IRS does not agree with their position.

The Right to Appeal an IRS Decision in an Independent Forum

Taxpayers are entitled to a fair and impartial administrative appeal of most IRS decisions, including many penalties, and have the right to receive a written response regarding the Office of Appeals' decision. Taxpayers generally have the right to take their cases to court.

The Right to Finality

Taxpayers have the right to know the maximum amount of time they must challenge the IRS's position as well as the maximum amount of time the IRS has to audit a particular tax year or collect a tax debt. Taxpayers have the right to know when the IRS has finished an audit.

The Right to Privacy

Taxpayers have the right to expect that any IRS inquiry, examination, or enforcement action will comply with the law and be no more intrusive than necessary, and will respect all due process rights, including search and seizure protections and will provide, where applicable, a collection due process hearing.

The Right to Confidentiality

Taxpayers have the right to expect that any information they provide to the IRS will not be disclosed unless authorized by the taxpayer or by law. Taxpayers have the right to expect appropriate action will be taken against employees, return preparers, and others who wrongfully use or disclose taxpayer return information.

The Right to Retain Representation

Taxpayers have the right to retain an authorized representative of their choice to represent them in their dealings with the IRS. Taxpayers have the right to seek assistance from a Low-Income Taxpayer Clinic if they cannot afford representation.

The Right to a Fair and Just Tax System

Taxpayers have the right to expect the tax system to consider facts and circumstances that might affect their underlying liabilities, ability to pay, or ability to provide information timely. Taxpayers have the right to receive assistance from the Taxpayer Advocate Service if they are experiencing financial difficulty or if the IRS has not resolved their tax issues properly and timely through its normal channels.

As you can see, you do have rights as a taxpayer! I like the one that talks about the "right to quality customer service." See, if an IRS employee ever screams, cusses, or in any way disrespects you, you have the right to ask for that person's supervisor's information.

Yes, every IRS employee is accountable to a supervisor. If you ever encounter an irate or rude IRS employee, you have the right to ask to speak to a different person.

You can also call them out on stuff. I spoke to an IRS representative who told me that I needed to mail my client's information. I replied, "don't you have a fax number?" He said he forgot and to go ahead and fax the information.

Yes, IRS employees ARE human and make mistakes. Just like others you know, they don't always get it right. So, don't be afraid to call out the IRS!

The IRS also makes billing errors. This is one of your most important rights as a taxpayer. I'd estimate that a solid 50% of tax bills have errors on them. Those are errors that the IRS usually fixes. But, they only do so when we fight them.

Sometimes it's worth reminding the IRS that you have rights as a taxpayer.

Interacting with IRS Employees

Correspondence sent to you by the IRS must give you a way to reply to it. If you get a letter that demands you mail a payment to the IRS today or pay via Western Union or money order to a specific address, without providing a phone number or person to talk to, you've just been scammed.

Each IRS letter will give you at least a phone number, fax number and mailing address to reply. If the letter doesn't have any contact information, it's best to get a professional to check it out for you.

I've had 25 clients in the past 2 years contact me and tell me that they got a call from the IRS demanding immediate payment by credit card or a warrant would be issued for that person's arrest. Total scam. Don't believe it for a New York minute! If you didn't know, that's 37 seconds.

Just don't, and I say again, don't ignore IRS letters! Doing so is like ignoring pain in your body. Yes, you can pop a pill to numb it for a little while. But, in the long run, it only leads to major health complications.

Don't do that!

Act on IRS letters before the deadline. Treat IRS notices like a bill that must be paid, or something will be shut off. In this case, your life can be shut off because IRS can go after all your assets, bank accounts, retirement accounts, etc.

I can't tell you the number of times I "beat that horse dead" telling clients to get their rears into gear. Sometimes my pleas work, sometimes they don't work. Nevertheless, it's worth spending time and effort to try to get through to those folks. Hopefully, you're not them 😊.

When trying to resolve a tax problem it's best to stay the course because it can take the better part of a year. The IRS doesn't begin working hours thinking of you as highest on their priority list. They just don't. Know that they'll eventually get around to notifying you of the information needed from you. Just don't hold your breath.

By following these tips you'll be better positioned to reduce your tax debt and resolve it. In chapter 2 we'll explore your resolution options.

<u>Incredible FREE Gift Offer!</u>

Visit <u>www.SacramentoTaxResolution.com</u> to get your FREE Tax Debt Consultation, a $495 value.

1. From the home page, enter your info where it says, "Do you owe any IRS or state taxes?"

2. Answer the questions.

Voila! Someone from my office will reach out to you!

"I was very skeptical at first that this business could help me with my IRS back taxes. I owed $39,000 and was stressed out. I contacted Mike and his team and began the process. It was very simple and straightforward. Mike's team was very professional and attentive to my concerns. Sacramento Tax Resolution was able to get the IRS to agree to an Offer in Compromise for $6,400! I would highly recommend them to anyone who is struggling to deal with back taxes. Sacramento Tax Resolution made the impossible to a reality and a skeptic

to a believer! Thank you, Mike, and your incredible team."-
Juan Vargas

Chapter 2:

Tax Resolution Options

When you're trying to resolve tax matters with the IRS, you have several different options.

Big Option 1 – Full pay the tax owed.

While seldom a popular option, it's a guaranteed way to solve your IRS problem. Although this will get the IRS off your back, it may not be the best option for you. If you have more than enough assets to fully pay the taxes due this may be your only option. If you don't have loads of cash or a garage full of Maseratis, you have other options. Keep reading.

Big Option 2 – Filing unfiled tax returns and replacing Substitute for Tax Returns

When resolving a tax problem, it is relatively common to have unfiled back tax returns. When you haven't filed tax returns in several years, many times the IRS files tax returns for you. Know that the tax returns they file for you are based on their estimates of your tax deductions and credits.

In many cases, those Substitutes for Returns (SFR for short) don't include ANY tax deductions or tax credits. For tax years up to 2017, they may not even give you credit for you, your spouse if married, or dependents. So, it's best to look seriously at filing actual tax returns. You know, the kind that includes tax deductions and tax credits.

Doing this option alone has been shown to significantly reduce your tax liability. I've seen clients go from owing nearly $100,000, to owing only $50,000, just by filing past due tax returns. Even if this means hunting down tax information from prior years, it'll most likely be worth your while.

It'll also mean that the IRS notices will become less and less frequent because you've tackled the tax return filing requirements.

Big Option 3 – Dispute the tax on technical grounds.

If there is a technical basis to dispute the amount of tax owed, you can call IRS out on it. You can claim that the return didn't include all of the tax credits and tax deductions you qualified for. In that case, it's best to file amended tax returns for all those tax years and include the tax credits and tax deductions.

You can also have another set of eyes look at your tax return. Maybe you had someone else file your tax return for you or you filed it yourself. In either case, I've been able to save clients a solid $2,000 per tax return.

Some quick math: if you have five years of unfiled tax returns and each results in a $2,000 benefit, you've just reduced your total balance owed by $10 grand. That's nothing to sneeze at. You only have two years from the date you paid the tax liability or three years from the date you filed the original return, whichever is later, to claim a refund.

If you file an amended return later than that time frame, the IRS will simply credit your account, lowering your total tax bill.

Big Option 4 – Currently Not Collectible Status (CNC)

If you do not have enough income and assets to cover the total tax liability or establish a reasonable monthly payment plan, you may qualify for Currently Not Collectible Status.

According to the IRS:

- A hardship exists if a taxpayer is unable to pay reasonable basic living expenses.

- The basis for a hardship determination is from information about the taxpayer's financial condition provided on Form 433–A, *Collection Information Statement for Wage Earners and Self-Employed Individuals* or Form 433–B, *Collection Information Statement for Businesses.*

- Generally, these cases involve no income or assets, no equity in assets or insufficient income to make any payment without causing hardship.

- An account should not be reported as CNC if the taxpayer has income or equity in assets and enforced collection of the income or assets would not cause hardship.

For individual taxpayers, this means that you currently don't make enough income to pay basic living expenses and pay the IRS any monthly amount. The IRS has their allowable standards posted on their website: https://www.irs.gov/pub/irs-utl/national_standards.pdf

You'll notice that the IRS considers your rent, utilities, transportation, groceries, etc. They'll also consider any debts you pay on such as credit cards, car loan, personal loans, etc. If your employer regularly lays you off, such as in the construction industry, it's in your best interest to do some tax strategizing. Wait until you're unemployed, then request Currently Not Collectible Status for those months.

Once you're back to work, it's a much better idea to explore other resolution options. See, the penalties and interest continue to accrue during CNC. And those penalties and interest can really add up. You'd then be in violation of the terms of your agreement because your IRS debt "snowballs." If you've been laid off, undergone major surgery, or experienced a debilitating illness, CNC is your best option.

If you're elderly and don't plan to return to work, you can request CNC status and wait for the Collection Statute Expiration Date (CSED) to expire. The CSED is typically 10 years from the date the tax was assessed. Check your IRS transcript to determine the CSED for each tax year. Know that if you setup a resolution option with IRS and then defaulted, the CSED is 10 years from the date IRS determined you defaulted.

So, don't think that you're in the clear because the tax was assessed on January 1, 2005, and it's been well past the CSED. If you setup a payment plan but IRS determined you defaulted on that payment plan on January 20, 2017, the new CSED is January 20, 2027. Those CSEDs are really important! I helped Don work out CNC status. He only earns $700 per month in Social Security Benefits and doesn't plan on returning to work due to an illness. He plans to wait out the CSED and eventually retire.

During CNC, you must remain current with any income tax return filing requirements. So, if you earned enough income to have a tax return filing requirement, be sure that you stay "current and compliant." You don't want to get an unexpected IRS letter telling you they're cancelling your CNC status!

For businesses, it's a little complicated because every business has some seasonality to it. Landscaping businesses are busiest during the warm months. Wedding businesses are busiest during summer. Restaurants are busiest when It's important to note that during football season and so forth.

If you owe payroll taxes, it's even more complicated. IRS prefers to shut down your business and go after the owners, shareholders and officers. Obviously, if your business can catch up via a payment plan and your business's revenue hasn't been rapidly declining, the payment plan is the way to go.

It's best to determine when your business is slowest. Doing so provides you the best chance of getting the IRS to agree to grant you Currently Not Collectible Status. However, just be aware that convincing an IRS agent to grant CNC is harder than trying to teach a 4-year-old quantum physics!

To request CNC, you'd need to contact the IRS and grant them the financial documents listed in their *Financial Analysis Handbook*. You'd also need to complete form 433-A for individuals and 433-B for businesses. This is an in-depth form that covers everything from your bank accounts and assets to your monthly expenses. We'll delve deep into this form in a later chapter, including which information to include on it.

If you don't feel comfortable talking to the IRS, please hire someone competent AND local! I'd recommend you hired me 😊. Even if you go with another firm, you can't go wrong with

33

hiring someone in your area. Someone you can look in the eye, shake his/her hand, and see in person to get your questions answered.

Don't put yourself in the unfortunate position of my clients Rob and Eva who hired an out-of-the-are firm that did nothing but take their money and run!

Big Option 5 – Installment Agreements

Most IRS tax debt cases are resolved through an appropriate payment plan. What?!? No mention of "pennies on the dollar," settle your $275,000 IRS debt for $10?

Nope. At least, not yet.

As of this writing, unemployment is at an all-time low. This means that most taxpayers and businesses won't qualify for the most heavily advertised IRS programs. If any tax professional tells you that you qualify for an offer in compromise or pressures you into doing something, you're totally ignorant of, without taking the time to explain it you in everyday English, don't walk, run.

Seriously.

If that firm doesn't respect you don't do business with them. I respect you. That's why I'm going to lay out the payment plan process in the following sentences.

An installment agreement is just a fancy way of saying a payment plan. This means that you simply arrange to pay your IRS taxes in bite-sized monthly payments. As long as the total is paid within 72 months, IRS usually will grant you the payment plan.

This depends on a couple of factors. First, do you owe IRS over $50,000? Second, do you have sufficient income and assets to full pay the taxes owed? If you fit both categories, they're going to want you to sell something to pay off the taxes. If you don't fit either category, there's an excellent chance you'll get approved for an affordable monthly payment.

If you owe over $50,000, the IRS will want financial documents from you and a completed form 433-A for individuals and 433-B for businesses. The IRS will mail you a letter within 30 days of your requesting a payment plan to notify you that they've approved your payment plan and all the pertinent details.

Keep paying your monthly payment and they'll stay out of your hair. Default on your payment plan and they'll come after you with a vengeance. Not necessarily right away, especially if you owe less than $50,000. But they'll catch up to you.

Big Option 6 – The Offer in Compromise

The IRS Offer in Compromise program is *the* most heavily advertised IRS program. That's because it's the sexiest of the bunch. I mean, come on, who doesn't want to pay a small fraction of the total taxes owed?

Right.

Everyone wants to settle for less than they owe. And that's why everyone and their mom brags that they can settle your IRS debt for less than you owe. Last I checked, around 5% of all IRS back tax cases are settled via the offer in compromise.

So, your odds aren't good. You'd need to be experiencing financial hardship. The good news is if you ARE experiencing financial hardship, the odds are good that IRS will agree to wipe out a whole bunch of your tax debt. I recently got Randal approved for an offer in compromise of $1,200. This wiped out over $150,000 in IRS debt.

It's possible.

Just don't go in thinking you're a candidate for this program. The reason those firms mention it is because it's the most appealing option. You must pay a $186 application fee unless you qualify for the "low-income certification."

That's when your income is so low that the IRS waives the application fee for you.

Big Option 7 – Penalty Abatements

Penalties typically make up 25% to as much as 50% of the tax liability. That said, it's important to look at how much each penalty adds to the total tax bill.

It adds up.

One of the first things to consider is getting IRS to forgive some of those penalties based on reasonable cause. Some of those reasonable causes are illness, unemployment, divorce and death of a spouse. There ARE things you can do to get your tax balance reduced.

One of the first things I recommend, even before negotiating a settlement with the IRS, is to get penalties removed. For example, you owe the IRS $75,000. Let's say $18,750 is penalties and interest. By getting the IRS to forgive even $10,000 of those penalties will lower your total balance to $65,000. Doing this alone will reduce your monthly payment by $135 or $1,620 per year.

Every little bit helps.

There is a way to get penalties and interest forgiven. But you need to ask.

Big Option 8 – Discharging taxes in bankruptcy

Contrary to popular belief, it is possible to discharge tax debts in bankruptcy. However, the taxes must be at least three years old. That means if the tax was charged on 12/31/2017, as of this writing, it's ineligible to be discharged. For instance, you file chapter 7 bankruptcy. If you file on 12/1/2019, the only taxes you can discharge are those filed in tax year 2015 and prior.

 The tax is considered charged at the end of that tax year. According to the IRS:

"The following tax debts (including interest) are not subject to discharge: taxes entitled to eighth priority, taxes for which no return was filed, taxes for which a return was filed late after 2 years before the bankruptcy petition was filed, taxes for which a fraudulent return was filed, and taxes that the debtor willfully attempted to evade or defeat.

Penalties in a chapter 7 case are dischargeable unless the event that gave rise to the penalty occurred within 3 years of the bankruptcy and the penalty relates to a tax that is not discharged. Only individuals may receive a discharge in chapter 7 cases; corporations and other entities do not."

Here's the deal: you've must file the past due tax returns, or the IRS must have filed a Substitute for Return (SFR) for those years you're attempting to discharge. Remember: the tax must have been charged. If you didn't file those tax returns, the tax may not have been charged. You wouldn't be able to get them wiped out in bankruptcy.

Big Option 9 – Innocent Spouse Relief

It is not uncommon to find yourself in trouble with the IRS because of your spouse or ex-spouses' actions. According to the IRS: "By requesting innocent spouse relief, you can be relieved of responsibility for paying tax, interest, and penalties if your spouse (or former spouse) improperly reported items or omitted items on your tax return.

Generally, the tax, interest, and penalties that qualify for relief can only be collected from your spouse (or former spouse). However, you are jointly and individually responsible for any tax, interest, and penalties that do not qualify for relief. The IRS can collect these amounts from either you or your spouse (or former spouse).

Innocent spouse relief only applies to individual income or self-employment taxes. For example, Household Employment taxes, Individual Shared Responsibility payments, and business taxes and trust fund recovery penalty for employment taxes are not eligible for innocent spouse relief.

The IRS will figure the tax you are responsible for after you file Form 8857. You are not required to figure this amount. But if you wish, you can figure it yourself.

You must meet all the following conditions to qualify for innocent spouse relief.

- You filed a joint return which has an understatement of tax due to erroneous items, defined below, of your spouse (or former spouse).

- You establish that at the time you signed the joint return you did not know, and had no reason to know, that there was an understatement of tax. See Actual Knowledge or Reason to Know, defined below.

- Considering all the facts and circumstances, it would be unfair to hold you liable for the understatement of tax.

- You and your spouse (or former spouse) have not transferred property to one another as part of a fraudulent scheme. A fraudulent scheme includes a scheme to defraud the IRS or another third party, such as a creditor, ex-spouse, or business partner.

Erroneous Items

Erroneous items are either of the following.

- **Unreported income.** This is any gross income item received by your spouse (or former spouse) that is not reported.

- **Incorrect deduction, credit, or basis.** This is any improper deduction, credit, or property basis claimed by your spouse (or former spouse).

The following are examples of erroneous items.

- The expense for which the deduction is taken was never paid or incurred. For example, your spouse, a cash-basis taxpayer, deducted $10,000 of advertising expenses on Schedule C of your joint Form 1040, but never paid for any advertising.

- The expense does not qualify as a deductible expense. For example, your spouse claimed a business fee deduction of $10,000 that was for the payment of state fines. Fines are not deductible.

- No factual argument can be made to support the deductibility of the expense. For example, your spouse claimed $4,000 for security costs related to a home office, which were actually veterinary and food costs for your family's two dogs."

Make sure that you correctly file the Innocent Spouse Relief claim because you may receive a reject notice from IRS if you don't. it's important to note that you'd need to have a compelling reason for claiming Innocent Spouse Relief. One of those reasons could be that you weren't involved in your spouse's business. Since you weren't directly involved, you didn't have firsthand knowledge of how the finances were managed.

In that case, your reason would qualify for Innocent Spouse Relief consideration.

Big Option 10 – Expiration of the Collection Statute (CSED)

The IRS only has a limited time during which to collect back taxes from you. This period starts on the date the tax was assessed or charged. For instance, your tax transcript shows that the tax was charged on February 10, 2017. This means the IRS has 10 years from that date to collect from you.

Should you bypass your option to file bankruptcy or don't qualify for other resolution options such as an offer in compromise, you can wait out the Collection Statute Expiration Date. Once that date comes, IRS can no longer collect those taxes from you.

Watch out!

You may accidentally extend the CSED by making a payment on that year's taxes owed, establishing a payment plan then later defaulting, filing for Innocent Spouse Relief, and even a payment plan can extend the CSED.

As you can see, you DO have options! Don't feel that your situation is hopeless. I talk to taxpayers and small business owners, just like you, who I've successfully helped get the IRS off their backs. There's hope. In chapter 3, I'll cover your options for securing representation before the IRS.

<u>Incredible FREE Gift Offer!</u>

Visit <u>www.SacramentoTaxResolution.com</u> to get your FREE Tax Debt Consultation, a $495 value.

1. From the home page, enter your info where it says, "Do you owe any IRS or state taxes?"

2. Answer the questions.

Voila! Someone from my office will reach out to you!

"My experience with Sacramento Tax Resolution could not have been better. They are extremely knowledgeable and professional, and we were able to resolve our serious tax issue with the IRS with zero money paid to the IRS. Thanks so much STR for all the support and a job well done."

-Michael Curtin

Chapter 3:

Determining When You Need Professional Assistance

You always have the option of representing yourself. It's totally your call. Some people are comfortable navigating the bureaucracy that is our tax code. In some instances, I RECOMMEND representing yourself. Say you owe the IRS $5,000. I'd certainly advise you to call them up and arrange a payment plan.

Enough said.

Since your balance is so small, IRS will automatically grant you a payment plan. Or, in the situation when you just need to get information to the IRS, or they messed up on filing your claim for refund. Self-represent.

However, when your situation is monstrous such as you owe at least $10,000, I'd advise you to hire someone to represent you. Just like with repairing your car, if you have the time, the money and the patience to learn it yourself go ahead and do it yourself. More power to you. But, if you'd rather not chance it, hire it out.

I'd prefer to hire someone to do it rather than learn it. If you work in a high-pressure, high stakes job, it's in your best interest to hire someone to represent you. If you're flat broke, represent yourself.

You see where I'm going with this?

As the late, great Zig Ziglar said, "If you have a tax problem, why not go a tax expert? Because you could become one, but it'd take years. And it's much easier to let him do it."

How to Select the Best Tax Consulting Firm

When choosing a firm that will represent you before the IRS, it's important that you hire local. I don't care if that firm claims to walk on water, if you can't see them, shake their hands, and visit their office, hire another firm.

 If the firm's office is in another part of the country and they only make the occasional trek into your area, hire another firm. If your gut instinct is to hire someone else, go with your gut.

Make sure they have a solid track record. Ask for client testimonials and success stories. Ask about their recent cases. If their most recent case was from the Reagan Era, hire another firm.

Tax Professionals to Consider

Make sure it's an Enrolled Agent. Why an Enrolled Agent, EA for short, rather than a CPA? Let's see.

 Most CPAs are great accountants. Your business needs audited financials, a review of your financials, or needs to establish an accounting system, go with a CPA. That person will run circles around an EA. You run an international conglomerate that needs to hire a controller, go with a CPA.

 I love CPAs.

But, if you have a tax problem, hire an Enrolled Agent. Why? Because tax is what we do. We focus on taxation. We've achieved the highest tax license awarded by the IRS. And we're the only tax professionals licensed by the IRS, as opposed to a state.

We advise, represent, and prepare tax returns for individuals, partnerships, corporations, estates, trusts, and any entities with tax-reporting requirements. Enrolled Agents' expertise in the continually changing field of taxation enables us to effectively represent taxpayers audited by the IRS.

So, there you have it.

Got an accounting problem? Go to a CPA. Got a tax problem? Go to an EA. Notice I didn't recommend tax attorneys? Why not? Simply stated: most tax attorneys don't represent taxpayers and small business owners before the IRS. When you have a tax fraud or criminal tax matter, go to an attorney. Or if you're Wesley Snipes or Paul Manafort.

Otherwise, an EA will suit you just fine.

How to Save on Professional Fees

The single greatest advantage of representing yourself in front of the IRS is that you save dinero! Don't, and I repeat, don't go the cheap route! Seriously, with something as sensitive as your financial situation, would you really look for the cheapest option? Isn't it worth it to get the best representation? If you needed braces, would you go to the guy advertising the cheapest price on Craigslist or the guy with a million success stories? Then, why would you entrust your most-sensitive information to the guy offering you a $99 special?

Really?

How to Find a Tax Professional

Ask your professional advisors. Your accountant or attorney may have someone in mind. Many of my clients are referred by their tax professional, attorney, or real estate agent. Check out their references. Do your due diligence. Again: make sure they're local!

Personal Referrals

Do you have a friend or acquaintance who has gone through tax problems with good results? His or her advisor may be a realtor, attorney, CPA, or other type of professional.

Tax Resolution Resource

To help you find the best possible IRS Representation, email me at: Mike@SacramentoTaxResolution.com

I Guarantee to bust my butt to properly represent you...or you don't pay me a dime! Let's talk today.

"I found Mike to be very knowledgeable and helpful. He takes the stress out of taxes and keeps you informed. I would recommend Mike to my family and friends without hesitation."-**James Curtis**

Chapter 4:

Nasty Things the IRS Can Do to You

The IRS has a lot of power when it comes to *enforced* collection, which means that they can make your life a living hell! Their power under federal law to collect the taxes owed is virtually unlimited. It's in your best interest to not PRO-crastinate. Yes, I hyphenated that word on purpose. Many people with back taxes are professionals when it comes to putting off for tomorrow what should be done today.

I can't begin to tell you how many people I've talked to who I'm still waiting on information from. Alas, I don't have the time or desire to babysit anybody. So, the continue accumulating IRS penalties and interest because they fail to act! This chapter is not intended to scare you. At least, not too much.

I've learned that it's either pain or fear that motivates people to act. In this case, when people learn about the things the IRS can, and will, do to them, only then do they take action. That's my goal—get you to take action. Following are some of the worst things the IRS can do to make your life a dreaded nightmare.

Federal Tax Liens

Once the IRS makes a valid assessment against you, they can file a federal tax lien. The thing that makes a federal tax lien so bad is that it attaches to all your bank accounts, retirement accounts and other assets. If you try to sell an asset, the IRS gets their cut first.

Oh yeah. A federal tax lien on your credit report also means that you can't do things like buy a home, buy a car, or qualify for low interest rates. Essentially, a federal tax lien makes lenders run the other way. Yes, it's bad.

The process for getting the tax lien removed is long. It's typically a 90-day process because the IRS wants to guarantee that they'll get paid. The IRS is just like us—they like getting paid.

The federal tax lien makes sure they can do just that.

Certificate of Discharge

A Certificate of Discharge (COD) is when the IRS releases a specific property from being covered by a federal tax lien. Notice that it's only one property, not all the properties you own. The IRS will grant a certificate of discharge on a specific property if:

1. The tax debtor will still have more equity in assets than the tax debt amount.

2. The property is under water on the mortgages.

3. The IRS lien position is such that they won't get any money anyway.

4. The buyer puts up a bond for the IRS' claim in the property.

5. Sale proceeds are escrowed, and the IRS gets paid at or after closing.

Lien Subordination

A lien subordination is when the IRS makes the federal tax junior to other debtors. Banks don't like this. They want to be the ONLY debtor of record. The IRS will voluntary put itself into a junior lien position if:

1. The IRS will get some money now.

2. The IRS will get some or all their money later as a result of the refinance.

3. If the refinance lowers the borrower's cost of living it benefits the IRS.

Bottom line: if it benefits the IRS, they'll allow a lien subordination.

Lien Withdrawal

If a case can be made that the withdrawal of the lien will facilitate payment of the tax liability, I can obtain a lien withdrawal. If I can demonstrate that the lien was filed in error. Now, you know that the IRS *never* makes a mistake, right? The IRS DOES make mistakes on a regular basis.

If the debt is being paid under one of a few different types of IRS payment plans they'll grant a lien withdrawal. It usually takes 3 consecutive payments on the payment plan before the IRS will issue a lien withdrawal because they're looking to determine if you're a risk to them.

Certificate of Release of Paid or Unenforceable Lien

The IRS is required to issue a certificate of release of lien no later than 30 days after the tax debt is paid in full. Once you pay the taxes in full, the lien must be released within 30 days. Here's the thing: YOU must request the lien withdrawal. IRS doesn't automatically grant it. At least not in the cases I've seen. You'd be really surprised to know that you're not the IRS's #1 priority. Surprising, I know.

If your relative died, the lien becomes unenforceable because the tax they owed died with them. Now, there can be grounds for the IRS to attempt to collect from the estate. And that's why there are resolution options even for estates.

Bank Account Levies

An IRS levy is the actual action taken by the IRS to get as much cash from your bank accounts as possible. I've seen situations when the taxpayer went to withdraw cash from the ATM, only to find that the bank balance was less than zero! Yes, once the IRS issues the CP504, *Notice of Intent to Levy,* they really mean that they plan to clear out your bank account(s)!

Don't ignore that warning notice! I mean, you could. But, doing so could bankrupt you.

Personal Property Levies

The IRS's levy power is extremely broad and includes the ability to force you to sell assets. They can go into the equity of a personal property and seize it before it has the chance to touch your hands.

You name it, the IRS can claim it. Cars, trucks, real property and any other assets of value. It's true that the IRS uses the seizure of assets only as a last resort. But it's also true that they do reserve the right to take your stuff if you don't make good on your tax bill.

Seizures

The IRS seizure of homes and business assets is much rarer than it used to be but does still happen. The IRS reserves the right to seize assets, auction them off, and use the proceeds to pay down the tax debt owed. Of course, this will only happen when you owe them $100,000 or more. Otherwise, it's not worth their expenditure of time and resources because taxpayers and business owners who owe less than six figures usually don't own enough assets to be worth seizing.

Wage Garnishments

The IRS wage garnishment is when the IRS issues a notice to your employer that you owe back taxes and their right to a portion of your wages. Yes, the IRS knows where you work! You can't hide from them.

If you don't make arrangements to pay the back taxes owed, the IRS will give you time to pay the balance or make arrangements to pay over time.

Fair Debt Collection Practices Act

The IRS is subject to the conditions of the Fair Debt Collection Practices Act just like any other debt collector. This Act includes:

(a) Abusive practices

There is abundant evidence of the use of abusive, deceptive, and unfair debt collection practices by many debt collectors.

Abusive debt collection practices contribute to the number of personal bankruptcies, to marital instability, to the loss of jobs, and to invasions of individual privacy.

(b) Inadequacy of laws

Existing laws and procedures for redressing these injuries are inadequate to protect consumers.

(c) Available non-abusive collection methods

Means other than misrepresentation or other abusive debt collection practices are available for the effective collection of debts.

(d) Interstate commerce

Abusive debt collection practices are carried on to a substantial extent in interstate commerce and through means and instrumentalities of such commerce. Even where abusive debt collection practices are purely intrastate in character, they nevertheless directly affect interstate commerce.

(e) Purposes

It is the purpose of this subchapter to eliminate abusive debt collection practices by debt collectors, to ensure that those debt collectors who refrain from using abusive debt collection practices are not competitively disadvantaged, and to promote consistent State action to protect consumers against debt collection abuses.

<u>Incredible FREE Gift Offer!</u>

Visit www.SacramentoTaxResolution.com to get your FREE Tax Debt Consultation, a $495 value.

1. From the home page, enter your info where it says, "Do you owe any IRS or state taxes?"

2. Answer the questions.

Voila! Someone from my office will reach out to you!

"I've enjoyed working with you very much because it takes the pressure off me. I was able to deal with someone in person. I felt satisfied with what I needed to have done. I was able to get my taxes done and take a load off my mind. It was the one thing in my life that was unresolved. I think, from this point forward, I can enjoy my life a little bit more."-**Bruce Johnson**

Chapter 5:

Minimizing Your Tax Bill: It All Starts with Your Tax Returns

Penalties and interest arise from filing income or payroll tax returns late, paying a balance late or not paying a balance owed in full.

Your Personal Income Tax Return

Here's a rough breakdown of how to compute the tax return:

Income:

Adjusted gross income minus

Standard or itemized deduction minus

Total payments & refundable credits

=*Refund or Amount You Owe*

This book won't go over *how* to accurately prepare your income or payroll tax returns. Many other books have been written on that subject. And I don't have the space to go over every facet of preparing income and payroll tax returns here.

Bottom line: Don't be shy, claim EVERY tax benefit you're legally entitled to!

Tax Resolution Resource

Call my office at 866-859-6420 for FREE tax advice.

Chapter 6:

Understanding IRS Collections and the Resolution Process

The U.S. Internal Revenue Service is the single largest collections agency in the world. In 2017, according to the IRS Data Book, the IRS collected a total of $3.4 trillion dollars! That's a whole bunch of dinero.

The IRS has unlimited power under federal law to collect back taxes. That doesn't mean that they'll skip all the steps and come after all you hold dear. They'll go through the proper channels to collect, usually.

But collect they will.

The only reason you need to be afraid of the IRS is if you're avoiding their letters. So long as you respond to them timely, you're fine.

Who am I kidding? You're reading this *because* you're avoiding the IRS! Keep reading.

Collections Starts with A Tax Deficiency

The IRS operates on a standard notice cycle. You get a bill. In about 30 days, if you didn't reply to the first bill, you get a bill saying something like you didn't pay your tax bill. Then you get another bill demanding payment.

Then they threaten to file a federal tax lien. Then the IRS files a federal tax lien as a claim against any assets you own. The federal tax lien prevents you from buying a home, refinancing your mortgage loan, or other financial moves.

It stays on your credit report until you plan to pay the IRS and pay them. The IRS won't take your word for it. You've got to make good on your payment arrangement.

Notice of Federal Tax Lien Filing (Form 668-Y)

If you fail to pay your tax bill the IRS files a notice of federal tax lien with your state or county of residence. This tax lien attaches to all assets you own. This includes retirement accounts, automobiles, and real property.

Attaches to everything you own or will own, including cash. And after 180 it supersedes most other types of liens except property taxes and mortgages.

You cannot sell, or transfer property covered by the lien (which is everything) without requesting a Certificate of Discharge. When refinancing real estate, you must subordinate the lien to the new mortgage. But the IRS will want to get paid. So, don't expect them to get the lien completely removed.

Notice of Intent to Levy (Form Letter CP-504)

Approximately 30 days after the federal tax lien has been filed, the IRS notifies you that they intend to levy your bank accounts, wages, and other assets.

This makes your life extremely stressful because the IRS can go after those assets until you've paid them in full. Don't be surprised when you try to withdraw cash from the ATM and notice that you're overdrawn. It happens on a regular basis.

Final Notice of Intent to Levy (Letter 1058)

Exactly 30 days after a CP-504 is issued, you're going to receive a final notice of intent to levy. If you don't respond, the IRS will seize bank accounts and other assets.

It's awkward when you're looking forward to payday, only to see that IRS took half of your paycheck! Don't let this happen to you. Friends don't let friends give the IRS their paycheck.

"Why was I levied?" you ask. Levies are usually used by IRS personnel as a "wake up call." Always respond to IRS notices on time and return phone calls from Revenue Officers. NEVER ignore them.

Alas, that's not the world we live in.

The good news: levies can be appealed through a special process. Expect to provide full financial information. You must demonstrate that the levy creates financial hardship. Banks must hold funds 21 days before sending to the IRS.

The Cycle Repeats

The notice cycle continues to repeat until you finally act. I talked to Saul, a self-employed drywall installer. He called in a panic because he came home to find an IRS agent's card and a note to call her immediately.

Can you imagine how that would feel? He was scared, to say the least. When I asked him how soon he could make it to my office, he said, "right away." Do you think he had a problem he was ready to solve? You betcha.

Revenue Officer Assignment

Your first time through this cycle your case gets assigned to a revenue officer. Those aren't the nicest people on the block, no sir. Those folks have been tasked with getting the money. Cue the Jerry Maguire, "show me the money clip."

They know that you've procrastinated replying to their friendly letters. Rejection hurts.

You've ignored their attempts to play nice. Kind of like that high school crush you wouldn't give the time of day. So, they come after you with a vengeance. Had you acted early in the notice cycle, it would've been a lot easier to deal with the IRS.

No, you waited. Until now.

The Tax Resolution Process

Whether your case is still assigned to ACS, or if it's been assigned to a Revenue Officer, there is a standard, step-by-step process by which your tax case gets resolved...

"What CAN'T you do? <u>I've sent an upbeat email to my friends telling them about your services.</u> If I ever come across anyone who needs tax services, I'll be sure to put in a plug for you."- **Mark Walsh**

Chapter 7:

Filing Unfiled Tax Returns and Replacing Substitute for Returns

Substitute for Returns (SFR) are tax returns prepared by the IRS based on their estimates of your tax situation. Those estimates are based on your past years tax returns.

Wait, what if your tax situation changed? Exactly. Everybody's tax situation changes sometimes. That's when it's best to replace those SFRs with accurate income tax or payroll tax returns. The IRS just guesses the numbers to put on those tax returns.

It's possible to drastically reduce the amount of back taxes owed just by filing tax returns to replace the SFRs. I've seen tax bills cut in half because the SFRs typically don't give you any tax credits or tax deductions. So, you can guess how that works out for you.

What's that, you say? You don't have the records from those years? Storage unit burned down? Ex-wife stole them and used them as kitty litter? Whatever.

According to the Taxpayer Advocate Service, "The Cohan rule is one of "indulgence" established in 1930 by the Court of Appeals for the Second Circuit in Cohan v. Commissioner.

The court held that the taxpayer's business expense deductions were not adequately substantiated but stated that" the Board should make as close an approximation as it can, bearing heavily if it chooses upon the taxpayer whose inexactitude is of his own making. But to allow nothing at all appears to us inconsistent with saying that something was spent."

The Cohan rule cannot be used in situations where IRC § 274(d) applies. Section 274(d) provides that unless a taxpayer complies with strict substantiation rules, no deductions are allowable for:

1. Travel expenses.

2. Entertainment, amusement, or recreation expenses.

3. Gifts; and

4. Certain "listed property."

A taxpayer must substantiate a claimed IRC § 274(d) expense with adequate records or sufficient evidence to establish the amount, time, place, and business purpose."

In human language, this means that it's possible to rack your brain and come up with expenses to the best of your ability. When you do this, you can reduce your tax bill substantially. It's important to act quickly, though.

If the IRS is knocking at your door, either literally or figuratively, don't delay another day. Act and get help immediately.

Tax Resolution Resource

For assistance in preparing your overdue tax returns, please visit www.SacramentoTaxResolution.com

Chapter 8:

The IRS Collection Information Statement

The Collection Information Statement is a financial instrument that the IRS uses to obtain current financial information necessary for determining how a wage earner or self-employed individual can satisfy an outstanding tax liability.

How to Fill Out Form 433

Each of the three different versions of the form ...

Section 1 - Business Information: This section is straight forward.

If you don't have information regarding the incorporation date, you can obtain that information from the Secretary of State's office or website.

Section 2 – Business Personnel and Contacts:

Please realize that whoever is listed as the "Person Responsible for Depositing the Payroll Taxes" may be investigated for the Trust Fund Recovery Penalty because that person was supposed to make sure the payroll taxes were paid but failed to do so.

Section 3 – Other Financial Information:

This series of questions all require a yes/no answer. Check the appropriate box. For each "yes," provide the details on the respective lines of that section.

Section 4 – Business Assets & Liabilities:

61

My clients tend to overestimate the value of their assets. They often think in terms of what they paid for something and what it would sell for brand new. That's not the correct information for this form's purposes.

Provide the fair market value of the asset. That's the number it would sell for at today's market rate. This is not the number you hope to sell the asset for. This number represents what a serious buyer would pay you today for it.

Also list any business liabilities and their account details.

Section 5 – Monthly Income and Expenses:

In essence, this section is a shortened Profit and Loss statement. It is the business's income and expenses.

IRS National Standards and Allowable Expenses

The income and expense section of the Collection Information Statement for individuals is the maximum amount of expense allowed for your area of the country. We'll go into each category.

National Standards for Transportation

The IRS sets national standards for transportation, including public transit, vehicle ownership costs, and vehicle operating costs.

National Standards for Food, Clothing, etc.

The IRS sets national standards for allowable expenses for the following typical household items:

-Food

-Housekeeping supplies. Includes cleaning products, toilet paper, etc.

-Apparel and services. This includes basic clothing and household services like lawn care.

-Personal care products and services. This includes haircuts, nail care, and other regular grooming expenses.

In the case when your regular expenses for any of those categories is more than the IRS's allowable standards, you can get away with the amount you pay. You'd just need to prove those expenses with receipts.

Health Care Costs

Taxpayers are also allowed to claim the actual cost of their health insurance premiums, plus out of pocket expenses like prescriptions, doctor visits, examinations, and procedures.

Housing and Utilities

For most families, the money they spend on putting a roof over their head. The IRS has standard allowances for these expenses, too. Again, if your housing and utility expense is more than the IRS's allowable standard for your area, you can claim the amount you pay. You'd just need to prove it.

Summary

It is important to claim every allowable expense because each dollar reduces your total tax liability. Don't be afraid to ask. It can't hurt. I always push the envelope for every possible expense. The worst the IRS can say is no.

Tax Resolution Resource

For up-to-date tables of IRS National Standards and allowable expenses for your local area, go to

https://www.irs.gov/businesses/small-businesses-self-employed/national-standards-food-clothing-and-other-items

Incredible FREE Gift Offer!

Visit www.SacramentoTaxResolution.com to get your FREE Tax Debt Consultation, a $495 value.

1. From the home page, enter your info where it says, "Do you owe any IRS or state taxes?"

2. Answer the questions.

Voila! Someone from my office will reach out to you!

"I wish I had learned about you sooner! It would've saved me the aggravation of hiring another firm and paying them thousands of dollars to do nothing for me."-**Vernon Nightwalker**

Chapter 9:

Installment Agreements (Payment Plans)

An Installment Agreement is a payment arrangement to pay the total tax liability you owe over a period as monthly payments. There are several different kinds of installment agreements.

Installment agreement benefits:

1. All nasty collections activity stops while IA request is being reviewed.

2. No collections activity while paying on it.

3. Potential lien removal under certain conditions.

4. Potential automatic penalty reduction

5. Seasonal adjustments if necessary.

6. May never have to pay the full amount you owe.

Downsides to installment agreements:

1. User fees: $105 for new; $45 reinstated; $52 for direct debit; $43 low income.

2. May need to provide extensive and invasive financial disclosure to IRS.

3. May need to provide extensive and invasive financial disclosure to IRS.

4. Penalties and interest still accrue.

5. May need to keep paying until statute of limitations runs out.

Pending status provides protection. To request an IA, you must provide:

1. Identifying information like name, social number or Employer ID number, etc.

2. Identify tax liabilities to be covered.

3. Proposed payment terms.

4. Have no unfiled returns and be up to date with estimated tax payments for current year.

Guaranteed Installment Agreements

If you owe $10,000 or less, not counting penalties and interest you qualify for a guaranteed installment agreement. The time limit is 36 months, within the statutory collection period. And this option is only available for income taxes, not payroll taxes. Getting one of these approved is as easy as calling the IRS. They don't require you to provide any financial information whatsoever.

They also won't file a federal tax lien against your assets, won't require you to sell assets, and doesn't require approval by an IRS supervisor.

Streamlined Installment Agreements

While not as "easy" as a Guaranteed Installment Agreement, there is another provision in the tax code for taxpayers that owe less than $50,000 including penalties and interest. This is available for any individual income tax situation and in business Income tax under $25k. For defunct businesses, it's available for any tax, over $25k for sole prop only.

Time Limit: 72 months within statutory time limit. The IRS will require partial financials for this type of installment agreement. Lien Filing is not required, but unlikely to be removed if already filed. Asset sale is not required. And IRS supervisor approval isn't required. But direct debit of a bank account is required when the total tax liability is $25,000 or more.

In-Business Trust Fund Installment Agreements

If you own a business that owes employment taxes No cap on the taxes, penalties and interest. Verification of income, expenses, assets and liabilities is not required if the total tax liability is less than $25,000 and paid in full within 5 years. If the total tax liability is more than $25,000 or the tax liability isn't paid in full within 60 months, the IRS will require full financial disclosure.

The IRS will file a tax lien for the total tax liability. And they can force you to sell off business assets. An IRS Revenue Officer WILL visit your business to physically inspect your business's assets. This could be an intimidating experience!

They'll require a corporate officer, shareholder or other responsible party, to determine whether there are any issues with the individual's tax compliance. In other words, the IRS will check that person's history of tax return filing, tax return payments, estimated tax payments, and other tax-related obligations. IBTF requires the sign off an IRS General Manager.

A pending installment agreement provides protection against IRS levy action, seizure of business assets, and shutdown of the business. If you plan on operating the business for many more years, it's a good idea to enter installment agreement as soon as possible.

Get three loan denial letters and be ready to produce proof of business asset valuation. That way, you're ready in case IRS asks for this proof.

Partial Payment Installment Agreements

A Partial Payment Installment Agreement (PPIA) is a payment plan where you pay less than the total amount owed. Legal limit up to 6 years.

This installment agreement is available for any type of tax and any amount of tax liability owed. The IRS will file a federal tax lien against your assets.

The IRS will require you to sell off assets to qualify for this type of installment agreement. This will require approval by an IRS supervisor. Trust Fund Recovery Penalty will be personally assessed if these are business payroll taxes. Consider an offer in compromise instead.

You or your business must be current with your tax return filings. And estimated tax payments need to be current. For payroll taxes, you must pay the next payroll tax deposit and not become delinquent again.

For PPIA, be ready for full investigation.

For IBTF, Regular, and PPIA, be ready to tap asset equity (this means taking out loans against property). Include all tax types and periods.

Helpful tips

1. Maximize your allowable expenses shown on form 433.

2. Try to borrow money against your assets.

3. Minimize income.

4. Take care of all tax accounts at the same time.

5. Never be afraid to ask for anything.

Incredible FREE Gift Offer!

Visit www.SacramentoTaxResolution.com to get your FREE Tax Debt Consultation, a $495 value.

1. From the home page, enter your info where it says, "Do you owe any IRS or state taxes?"

2. Answer the questions.

Voila! Someone from my office will reach out to you!

Chapter 10:

Currently Not Collectible Status (CNC)

If you are unable to pay the IRS anything, you may qualify for Currently Not Collectible Status. Just know that you'd basically need to be financially destitute to qualify for this resolution option. In other words, you're barely able to make ends meet with your current income.

Obviously, paying the IRS is out of the question.

The times I've seen clients get approved for CNC are:

Retirement. Under certain circumstances, your income goes down when you retire. That's the case for most retirees I talk to. Even if you've worked for your employer for 25 or 30 years, your pension will probably only be 60-80% of your base wage. Even when you include Social Security Benefits, you're looking at a decrease in income during retirement.

Disability. If you become disabled, your income definitely goes down. This puts you in a favorable position to settle with the IRS. Especially when you factor in the timeframe for remaining on disability, you're usually looking at a minimum of one year. That's the best chance of getting CNC approved.

Unemployment. Let's face it: when you're out of a job, your income decreases. Some industries are known for temporary unemployment like construction. I spoke to Lincoln, a construction worker who owes the IRS about $300,000. This guy has gone exempt from federal and state withholding for nearly ten years! As a result, he's put himself in a bind.

Now, he has a chance to be placed on CNC. But that'll only be granted if he chooses to live on rice and beans until his IRS issue is handled. Otherwise, it'll be an uphill battle.

Those are the most likely scenarios to qualify you for CNC. Just know that the penalties and interest continue to be charged. CNC is not the best option if you still have at least a decade left before retirement.

Bankruptcy. If you, or your business, files for bankruptcy, you can qualify for CNC. If the business has closed, you have a very good chance of getting approved for CNC.

The good news: there IS a way to get the IRS off your back. You must act, though. Don't think that anyone has the solution to your problem without your cooperation. I'm usually waiting on information from the client, not the other way around.

When I take on a client, I rock and roll with their case. They know exactly where the case stands. There's no guessing, wondering, or hoping that I do my job. They get notified every step of the way.

The IRS generally has 10 years to collect the taxes from the date the taxes were assessed. You can wait out the statute of limitations period. At which point, the IRS cannot collect the taxes owed from you. That is, of course, unless you do something to extend the statute of limitations like communicate with the IRS, setup a payment plan, etc.

Hence the importance of hiring trustworthy, competent representation. Don't do anything your rep advises you not to do. If you choose to ignore the rep's advice, you'll be the worse off for it.

"Wow! I had such an awesome experience with Mike and his staff, even though it was all virtual (due to COVID). He was instrumental in filing my taxes and getting me a refund when I was not expecting such a great outcome! His help was of such importance to me because I recently lost my husband to COVID and my husband."-**Lala Chappell**

"I have never had such a great experience with tax professionals as I am having with Sacramento Tax Resolution. Always quick to respond to any and all questions and we very scared when our bookkeeper for 23 years retired. I am at complete ease! thank you so much for you and all the team. AWESOME!"-**Angie Diamond**

"Wow! I thought I was going to owe the IRS a bundle. Thanks for turning that around into a refund." -**Amanda Morton**

"Mr. Ornelas has been a professional with timely response and great communication overall. Thank you for making filing our tax yes easier, especially for maximizing as 1099 work to save us quite a bit, and even educating us on valuable tax information. Thanks! Highly recommended."-**Rafael Remotigue**

Chapter 11:

Offer in Compromise Program

Whenever you hear the phrase "pennies on the dollar" the ad is referring to the Offer in Compromise Program or OIC, for short. This program is the most-widely marketed resolution option out there. Know that not everyone qualifies for this option. So, if you sit down to talk to a potential IRS representation firm, and all they do is tell you that you can settle for less than you owe, without doing any investigation of liability and financial analysis, don't walk, run!

Eligibility

Your eligibility to settle for less than what you owe is determined by your monthly income and expenses, plus assets and liabilities. If you have enough income after all expenses, you won't qualify for this option. If you have more than enough worth of assets to pay the tax liability in full, you won't qualify.

On the other hand, if you barely make ends meet, you may qualify. If you're insolvent, meaning, your liabilities are worth more than your assets, you may qualify. The best way to determine whether you qualify or not, is to sit down with a trustworthy tax advisor to run some calculations based on your financial situation.

Could you run the numbers yourself? Of course, you can. But you're better off hiring someone to do it for you because there are quite a few tricks to the trade. You can find out if the firm is reputable when they tell you that they need to conduct some research to determine your resolution options.

If all the firm does is push this option on you, run. Yes, they'll file the OIC for you. However, there's no way the OIC will be approved. There ARE firms like that out there. Buyer beware.

There are two different types of Offers in Compromise:

1. Periodic payment. This option allows you to offer the IRS less than what you owe but pay that amount in up to 24 installments. You end up paying way more with this option because you need to make payments even while the IRS is considering your Offer.

2. Lump sum. This option only requires you to pay the $186 application fee and a 20% down payment. You end up with up to a 50% lower total OIC amount than the periodic payment. While the OIC is pending, you don't have to make any payments to the IRS. Which allows you time to save up the rest of the money you offered IRS.

Either way, the process can take up to one year, sometimes even longer. While the OIC is processing, all IRS collection activity stops.

Application Process – What to Expect

When you file an OIC, a Process Examiner will determine how much is a reasonable offer. It's best to offer as little as possible because the worst IRS can do is fire back asking for more money. If the IRS accepts your first OIC amount, you could've offered less! That's why it's important to find someone who does this for a living.

That person will do a bang-up job for you because his/her livelihood depends on it.

By filing an OIC, you agree to the following for the next 5 years:

1. To stay current with your tax return filing (1040, 1120, 1120s, 940, 941)

2. To stay current with your estimated taxes and/or federal tax deposits

3. To timely pay any tax liability due or make a payment arrangement.

You must complete form 433-A(OIC). This form is like a loan application because it requires you to list your assets, liabilities, income and expenses. It's all inclusive. Be sure to include the item if you're in doubt. It's better to fully disclose than appear to hide information from the IRS.

The IRS has ways of finding out if you've hidden any assets or income items. It's best to be upfront about everything. The goal is to get back on the right track. Sometimes that means admitting hidden items. Remember: you're showing the IRS that you're going to be a good, little taxpayer. The first step in that process is honesty.

Some assets only require listing a "salvage value." That means that you don't list the amount you paid for the item. After all, if you bought a car three years ago, it's not going to fetch the price you paid for it.

Nope.

You'll get a lower price. So, only list 80% of the price you could sell the item for today. Use sites like KBB.com, Zillow, etc. It's unnecessary to hire a professional property, automobile, or precious metals appraiser. That's a little too much for our intents and purposes here.

Should you default on doing any of the above or a combination of the above the IRS CAN reject your OIC. Yes, even after 4 years! You're technically on tax probation. It's possible to go through the whole process of an OIC, only for IRS to reject it and come after you for the full amount of the tax, penalties and interest you originally owed.

The OIC process is not to be taken lightly. See, if you think the process only involves the IRS wiping out a bunch of taxes you owe, you're mistaken. This IS an agreement. Meaning you and the IRS must follow what you agree to. You can't think that your job is done just because your OIC is approved.

Nope.

You've got your work cut out for you over the next five years. It took you some time to get into trouble with the IRS. Allow time to get out of the trouble.

Appeals

If your OIC is rejected, you can appeal the rejection. It's your right under the Internal Revenue Code to submit an appeal to an IRS decision. You know what? For some reason, some of the kindest, most intelligent people work in the appeals division. Many times, an appeals officer will approve a previously rejected offer.

The appeals division doesn't ALWAYS approve a rejected offer, but it's worth a shot. While the OIC appeal is processing, the same collections hold applies as with an OIC that's processing. The collections hold gives you some breathing room between the originally filed appeal and when you need to pay.

Incredible FREE Gift Offer!

Visit www.SacramentoTaxResolution.com to get your FREE Tax Debt Consultation, a $495 value.

1. From the home page, enter your info where it says, "Do you owe any IRS or state taxes?"

2. Answer the questions.

Voila! Someone from my office will reach out to you!

Chapter 12:

Reducing IRS Penalties with Reasonable Cause Penalty Abatements

There are a lot of common misconceptions surrounding the abatement (removal) of IRS penalties and interest. Many of those misconceptions center around the idea that the IRS automatically forgives penalties. That's not true.

The IRS doesn't automatically forgive anything. It's dependent upon you to request penalty forgiveness. You need to have a good reason for doing so. Those good reasons are known as "reasonable cause." That's how the IRS words it, so that's what we'll call it here.

Reasonable Cause Criteria

The IRS charges dozens of different types of penalties. I've seen penalties comprise as much as 50% of balances owed to the IRS! That's a whole lot of moola.

Reasonable cause criteria include, but is not limited to:

1. Incorrect IRS advice you followed.

2. Incorrect tax preparer advice you followed.

3. Unemployment

4. Illness (yourself or a loved one)

5. Bankruptcy

The IRS requires that you state the reason why you're requesting penalty forgiveness. You can't just write the IRS and say, "forgive the penalties because I want you to." That won't count. Your best bet is to state the facts and circumstances surrounding the penalties. For example, on January 3, 2003, x happened. Then, I became unemployed on x date and didn't get a job until x date. Blah, blah, blah.

Give every possible detail you can reasonably think of. And stay on track. Don't give them a laundry list of things you did while unemployed like watch tv for seven hours per day, take out the trash once per week, etc. Only list those important details.

Writing Your Penalty Abatement Request

You can use Form 843, *Claim for Refund and Request for Abatement* to apply for relief from penalties. However, writing your own letter allows you to provide a detailed explanation of the facts and circumstances that led to the IRS charging those penalties.

Writing a letter also gives you more reasons to explain why the IRS should forgive the penalties. The form 843 only lists a limited number of reasons for asking the IRS to forgive penalties. You can go into all kinds of detail on your personal letter. A letter is the best way to go.

Where to Send Penalty Abatement Requests

If you have or recently had a Revenue Officer assigned to you then fax the penalty abatement request to the Revenue Officer. If you don't have the Revenue Officer's fax number, simply call him/her after normal business hours such as 8pm your time or anytime on the weekend. You'll get voicemail and hear the fax number to send that Revenue Officer your penalty abatement request.

If you do not have a Revenue Officer assigned to your case send your penalty abatement request to the address shown on the IRS notice. Make sure to properly label your penalty abatement request! Or else the IRS won't know what to do with your letter.

Penalty Abatement Review Process

The IRS will make a determination regarding the penalties to remove. They don't always remove all the penalties. My experience has shown they forgive 25%-100% of the penalties. Don't expect 100% to be wiped out. However, like the great Wayne Gretzky said, "you miss 100% of the shots you don't take."

In other words, even if you only get 25% of the penalties removed, at least it's something. It's much better than not asking and getting 0% of the penalties removed.

The process takes up to 12 weeks. Be patient. Your request is going to an IRS center that probably gets more mail than Santa Claus at Christmas time. You'll hear back from the IRS about their determination. If the penalty forgiveness triggers a credit balance on your IRS account, they'll mail you a refund check.

Oh, happy day!

Alas, if you still owe IRS back taxes after they've forgiven penalties, the number of penalties forgiven reduces your total balance owed.

For example, you owe $57,327.51. You petition the IRS for a penalty abatement. They agree to forgive $3,200 in penalties. The $3,200 is credited to your account because your total balance owed is $54,127.51.

Tax Resolution Resource #7

If you would like assistance in writing your penalty abatement request, please email me at:

Mike@SacramentoTaxResolution.com

"My husband and I really appreciate Mike for listening to our situation patiently and for sharing his knowledge during our initial consultation. He sounds like a nice person, not like those who pressure to sell their services. Thank you for your advice!"-**Naomi Sato**

"As the principal of a small business in California - I have gone through 2 EAs and 2 CPAs who have all filed my tax returns in-correctly with the IRS while also failing to file correct forms for the State of California. The result is $8,900 in penalties with the IRS and $5,000 with the State of California FTB. The FTB reviewed everything and confirmed that all CPAs and EAs whom I hired to file my taxes did NOT file correct. The FTB took mercy on me and now I got a consultation from Mike today and he was MAGNIFICENT in terms of his advisory. I strongly recommend him as I have experienced nothing but hubris and incompetency from so many CPAs and EAs. THANK YOU, MIKE - for your advice. I will pursue based on our consultation."-**Moe Montana**

"I have never had such a great experience with tax professionals as I am having with Sacramento Tax Resolution. Always quick to respond to any and all questions and we very scared when our bookkeeper for 23 years retired. I am at complete ease! thank you so much for you and all the team. AWESOME!"-**Angelina Jaurique**

"Mike was very professional and informative in handling our tax resolution. I would highly recommend Sacramento Tax Service. Thank you."-**John Veith**

"Mike, thank you for your assistance this afternoon. The material you shared before our appointment was extremely valuable. I truly appreciate your knowledge and suggestion regarding my situation, thank you."-**Paula Wiggins**

"Mike is an awesome guy who is very friendly and knows his work. He also is very knowledgeable and explains everything to you."-**Talib**

"Want someone with plenty of Tax experience to help you file your taxes & protect you from the IRS? Look no further..."-**Matt Nieschalk**

"I feel confident that your company is the right company to help me with my tax matter. I'm confident you can help me get my taxes handled."-**Bill Barhite**

"Mike was extremely helpful. He took the time to understand my situation in the initial consultation and gave me his honest opinion on how to move forward. He knows his stuff!"-**Stephanie Taylor**

"Michael was a great help to me he answered all questions that I needed he gave me websites to go to talk to IRS and how to do my paperwork for withholdings so I wouldn't own so much at the end of the year the year I love how they talk to you and communicate with you. Thank you so much."-**Naomi Hollins**

"First I wanna thank you from the bottom of my heart, you guys really went above and beyond. "If we can't help, we will not take your case", that's what made me call and I'm glad I did. A few minutes of your time, that's all it take, it can make a world of difference. Anyone with tax problems, call them. God bless and thank you."- **Sathiane Soulyalangsy**

"This is the place to go any IRS problems. All staff is very friendly and they are so helpful with tax purposes. Must see them first before go to anywhere."-**Kulwinder Singh**

Chapter 13:

Payroll Taxes

Payroll Taxes Are the Worst!

Many small businesses get in Cash Flow problems for all kinds of reasons. How they handle these problems, especially when payroll taxes are involved, usually determines if they stay in business or not. The IRS takes an extremely strong position on payroll tax violations. They would rather close the business and sell off all the assets instead of trying to work out a deal with the business.

The worst thing about business payroll taxes is that the IRS can collect business payroll taxes from anyone they think was responsible for not paying the taxes.

For example, the business owner or any check signer on the business bank account may be singled out for collection activity.

They will try everything to get these payroll taxes. Usually, a visit to your home or work is in order to start the collection procedures. Then all the weapons in their arsenal can be used (Liens, Levies, or Seizure) until the taxpayer has agreed to some type of repayment.

Once the IRS has determined that the business cannot pay the payroll taxes and they have turned their sights on the individuals they think are responsible...LOOK OUT!

Trust Fund Recovery Penalty (TFRP)

What is it? It's Social Security, Medicare, and income taxes held in "trust" for payment to the government. These are the employee's portion of the taxes.

Essentially, the government is trusting the business with holding its money for deposit later. That's why the business is required to setup a separate checking account solely for the deposit of payroll taxes. The government then withdraws what's owed to them from that account on a quarterly basis.

Who is Responsible for Paying Payroll Taxes?

According to Internal Revenue Manual §5.7.3.3.1: "Responsibility is a matter of status, duty, and authority. A determination of responsibility is dependent on the facts and circumstances of each case." The Internal Revenue Manual provides guidelines for determining the responsible person. But that definition is not always true.

Just because someone is an officer in the business, does not make that person responsible. The exception is the single member/shareholder LLC or S-Corporation. When it's a business where two spouses are handling the day-to-day operations, it's very difficult to prove one or the other spouse was solely responsible, for obvious reasons.

Bookkeepers. When a bookkeeper is concerned about his/her job at a small company, it's possible that person will make a bad choice. In this case, it's the neglect to timely deposit and pay the payroll taxes owed. This person chooses to withhold that information from the boss or owner. This bookkeeper has the status, duty, authority to process payroll and make federal tax deposits.

When this person chooses to not notify the business owner that he/she has chosen to not make timely federal tax deposits, the bookkeeper has become the willful and responsible person.

Third-party payroll service provider. If the payroll service doesn't make timely federal tax deposits, they are the willful and responsible party.

Limited partners/shareholders. For example, during the formation of partnership, the limited partner opens the business bank account. Several years later, the business defaults on making its federal tax deposits. The limited partner is listed as the person of record on the bank account. Now this person can be held liable for not making the timely federal tax deposits.

Responsible Person Duties

1. Hires employees

2. Fires employees

3. Makes federal tax deposits

4. Signs payroll checks

5. Has certain officer duties

6. Directs the actions of employees in any of the above matters

In general, authority for making federal tax deposits can be delegated but not responsibility. Was the person doing the delegating removed from responsibility by the delegation?

Establishing Willfulness

Was it done on purpose?

Was the responsible person aware of the failure to pay?

*Failure to correct the failure to pay proves willfulness. Once the owner becomes aware that the payroll taxes weren't paid, the owner becomes the willful and responsible person.

IRS Form 4180 lists this question: "were other bills paid by the business instead of the payroll taxes?" For instance, owner's salary, electric bill, etc.

Many business owners attempt to delay handling the defaulted payroll tax deposits. Be aware that the IRS is allocating resources to visit and attempt to secure anymore payroll tax deposit defaults.

Trust Fund Recovery Penalty Interview

This interview takes place either at the business location or over the phone. When only one person is willful and responsible, as in a single member LLC or S-Corp, the IRS Revenue Officer most likely won't get past page 1 of form 4180.

According to the Internal Revenue Manual, the IRS Revenue Officer is not allowed to accept a form 4180 completed by a representative. There ARE revenue officers who WILL accept written and completed forms by fax or mail.

If the IRS sends the representative or business owner form 4180, they are not required to complete it because the Internal Revenue Manual requires the revenue officer to personal interview the business owner. I never let a client complete the 4180-interview process without me present.

We complete form 4180 together, prior to the scheduled interview with the IRS. We then rehearse our defense beforehand.

Don't answer ANY questions by the IRS without me present if the IRS Revenue Officer calls or shows up. Never sign form 2751 accepting the proposed Trust Fund Recovery Penalty without a good reason. Otherwise, you lose any appeal rights and tax court rights.

60 days after the interview, the IRS automatically assesses the Trust Fund Recovery Penalty. But, there's no good reason to forfeit that extra time to resolve the matter.

How to Defend Against Assessment of the Trust Fund Recovery Penalty

I establish the facts and circumstances surrounding the operations of the business. The goal is to separate the responsibilities and duties of the owners and shareholders. I do this by doing my due diligence and conducting an in-depth investigation of liability and transcript analysis.

This process goes over all the information the IRS is looking for as they attempt to hold someone responsible for failing to timely deposit the payroll taxes due. It takes anywhere from 5 days to 10 days, depending on how soon the business owner provides all the information needed for this process.

The information needed to conduct the investigation of liability and transcript analysis is as follows:

☐ Articles of Incorporation, Articles of Organization, or Business License.

☐ Profit and Loss statement (P&L) covering year to date (YTD) or at least last 3 months.

☐ Copies of credit card merchant account statements of last 6 months.

☐ Copies of business bank account statements (including payroll and operating accounts) of last 6 months.

☐ Accounts receivable list (including what they owe you and how far behind they are in paying).

☐ Statements for any investment accounts held by the business (stocks, bonds, etc.).

☐ Statements for all business credit cards, loans, lines of credit, and other debts.

☐ Property tax bills/statements for all property owned by the business-most recent.

☐ Copies of all utility bills- most recent.

☐ Mortgage statements and commercial leases.

☐ Vehicle loan statements and copies of vehicle registrations (including trailers, backhoes, etc.)

☐ Description, purchase date, current value, and loan statements (if applicable) of all business machinery, merchandise inventory, tools, equipment, etc.

☐ Copies of any current UCC financing statements currently in effect.

☐ Copy of most recent annual business tax return (Form 1065, 1120, 1120S, etc.)

☐ Copy of most recent quarterly employment tax return (Form 941).

☐ Copy of most recent county and state sales tax returns.

Trust Fund Recovery Penalty Assessment Process

4180 Interview. This is the IRS's attempt to establish the willful and responsible party. When that's established, they proceed to determine who should have made the payroll tax deposits. If the IRS determines that every executive officer was responsible and willfully didn't make the timely payroll tax deposits, they will assess the trust fund recovery penalty on all those they deem responsible.

Payments made from the business towards the TFRP reduce the personal assessment. This is a business and personal tax liability because it gets assessed against the business and the individuals attached to the business the IRS deems willful and responsible in not making the payroll tax deposits.

Even if the business closes, the personal liability usually remains.

I've listed IRC §3505 in its entirety so you can see the exact parameters of the TFRP.

Liability for Direct Payment of Wages – IRC § 3505(a)

IRC § 3505(a) makes third parties personally liable for the payment of withholding taxes where they pay wages directly to employees of another.

IRC § 3505(a) applies to lenders, sureties, or other persons.

"Other persons" includes anyone similar to a lender or surety who pays the wages of employees of another out of its own funds. The most common situation in which a person other than a lender or surety (a statutory "other person") may be found liable under IRC § 3505(a) is where a prime or general contractor, out of necessity (to keep the employees of the subcontractor on the job) or by contract, pays net wages directly to employees of a subcontractor that is having financial problems.

IRC § 3505(a) does not apply to a person who is acting only as agent of the employer or as agent of the employees (such as a union agent). See Treas. Reg. § 31.3505-1(c) examples.

Liability under IRC § 3505(a) extends to withholding under:

IRC § 3402, withheld income taxes.

IRC § 3102, withheld FICA taxes; and

IRC § 3202, withheld railroad retirement taxes.

Liability does not extend to the employer's share of employment taxes; nor does liability extend to penalties that the Service may impose on the employer.

IRC § 3505(a) does not relieve an employer from responsibilities with respect to withholding taxes. The responsibilities continue even though a lender may be paying the employees' wages. The liability of the lender in such a case is to pay the taxes only where the employer does not do so.

The employer is obligated to file an employer's tax return (Form 941) and comply with other requirements generally imposed on employers.

The lender's liability is a sum equal to the taxes (together with interest) required to be deducted and withheld from the wages by the employer.

When evaluating whether wages are being paid directly, the Service and the courts look to the "substance" of the transaction and may find the direct payment of net wages present even though a " subterfuge" is used to disguise the substance of the arrangement. See United States v. Kennedy Construction Co. of NSB, Inc., 572 F.2d 492 (11th Cir. 1978) (subcontractor opened special payroll account out of which it issued payroll checks; however, the contractor provided the funds in the account after verifying the net wages owed each pay period and countersigned the pay checks).

5.17.7.2.2 (08-01-2010)

Liability When Funds are Supplied — IRC § 3505(b)

IRC § 3505(b) provides that a lender, surety, or other person who supplies funds to or for the account of an employer for the specific purpose of paying wages of the employees of such employer may be personally liable for any unpaid withholding taxes even though this person does not directly pay the employees' wages.

A person within the meaning of Section 3505(b) includes the following:

A prime or general contractor who supplies funds directly to a subcontractor to meet its net payroll with knowledge of the subcontractor's inability to pay its withholding taxes. United States. Algernon Blair, Inc., 441 F.2d 1379 (5th Cir. 1971).

A shareholder, including a parent company of a subsidiary, who makes a capital contribution or a direct loan, or who puts up collateral for a loan from a third party to a corporation if the loan is to be used by the corporation to pay net wages. United States v. Intercontinental Industries, Inc., 635 F.2d 1215 (6th Cir. 1980).

A bank that honors a customer's/employer's overdrafts for payroll checks. Fidelity Bank, N.A. v. United States, 616 F.2d 1181 (10th Cir. 1980).

Before a person can be liable under Section 3505(b), the following two conditions must exist.

The person must know that the advanced funds are to be used for the payment of wages; this does not include an "ordinary working capital loan." "Ordinary working capital loans" are ones that are made to enable the borrower to meet current obligations as they arise; they are not earmarked for any particular purpose.

Note: If the maker of an "ordinary capital loan" has actual notice or knowledge at the time of the advancement of funds that the funds or a portion of the funds are to be used to pay net wages, IRC § 3505(b) will apply regardless of whether the written agreement states that the funds were advanced for another purpose. Treas. Reg. § 3505-1(b)(3); United States v. Intercontinental Industries, Inc., 635 F.2d 1215 (6th Cir. 1980).

The supplier of funds must have "actual notice or knowledge " at the time such funds are advanced that the employer does not intend to or will not be able to make timely payment or deposit of taxes required to be withheld. The lender has actual notice or knowledge of any fact from the time such fact is brought to its attention or would have been brought to its attention if the organization had exercised due diligence. See United States v. Park Cities Bank and Trust Co., 481 F.2d 738 (5th Cir. 1973).

Note: The burden of establishing actual notice or knowledge in such cases is on the government.

It is the Service's position that notice to, or knowledge by, any agent of a third-party supplier of funds is imputed to the third party. This is true even if the agent conceals the facts from the supplier. United States v. Park Cities Bank and Trust Co., 481 F.2d 738 (5th Cir. 1973).

Under IRC § 3505(b), the liability of the third party may not exceed 25 percent of the amount supplied to the employer for the specific purpose of paying wages.

The 25% limitation applies to accrued interest. O'Hare v. United States, 878 F.2d 953 (6th Cir. 1989).

Example: A lender advances $100,000 to Employer A for the purpose of paying net wages. The employer fails to pay withholding taxes and is assessed a liability of $25,000 plus an additional $10,000 in accrued interest. The Service may file suit against the lender for $25,000, which is 25% of the amount supplied to the lender. If the assessment had been $20,000 plus an additional $10,000 in interest, the Service still could have sued for $25,000 ($20,000 in tax and $5,000 in accrued interest).

The lender's liability does not include penalties that the Service may impose on the employer.

The employer remains responsible for filing returns (Form 941).

Payments by the lender of withholding taxes reduces the liability of the employer. Similarly, payments by an employer of the withholding taxes reduces the liability of the lender.

Penalties

Failure to file penalty

5% per month

25% cap

Minimum of $135 or 100% of tax due, whichever is less.

Failure to pay.

.5% per month

25% cap

Federal Tax Deposit Penalty

1-5 days late: 2%

6-15 days late: 5%

16 days or more: 10%

Still unpaid 10 days after first bill: 15%

The Small Business/Self-Employment Division of the IRS considers the collection of payroll taxes one of their most important jobs. Payroll tax deposits are that important because it's the largest non-debt related source of United States Income. It represents nearly 40% of the United States' operating budget, according to the U.S. Treasury.

Internal Revenue Code Section 6672 allows the "corporate veil to be pierced in collection of payroll taxes." This means that someone in the corporation will be liable for a portion of the payroll tax debt. There's no avoiding the personal assessment of the civil penalty portion of the payroll tax penalties. The IRS wants someone on the hook for this portion of penalties. No exceptions.

Resolution options

There are various options available for settling the payroll tax debt not all of them apply to your business's situation. I'll cover all of them. Keep in mind that the facts and circumstances, goals for the future of the business, and other criteria will be required to be explored before you consider ANY resolution option.

Penalty Abatement (forgiveness)

There's usually a way to get penalties removed. This option is one of the first ones to explore. Penalties can comprise as much as 50% of the total payroll tax debt.

Since the penalties keep piling up, it's not unusual to have an original balance that's a small fraction of the total assessed balance. Requesting penalty abatement (forgiveness) is always a good idea. After all, worst case scenario is the IRS only agreeing to remove 10% of the penalties. That's 10% less payroll tax debt you must pay.

In Business Trust Fund Express (IBTFE) Installment Agreement

You won't be required to complete a form 433-B, Collection Information Statement for Businesses. This form lists your business's assets, liabilities and other financial information.

Taxes, penalties and interest must be less than $25,000. Also, you must apply for this option BEFORE your case is assigned to a local IRS Revenue Officer. Otherwise, this option isn't available to you. You must pay the balance in full within 24 months of the date of making this payment agreement. The final payment must be made prior to the collection statute expiration date. That's the last date the federal tax law allows the IRS to collect the taxes from your business.

Your payments must be made via direct debit of the business bank account if the total liability is more than $10,000. The debt can only include current and prior year calendar quarters. You must not have initiated 4180 interview proceedings prior to agreeing to the IBTFE. The 4180 interview relates to IRS Form 4180. On it are questions that the IRS Agent will take you through when you owe payroll taxes.

In Business Trust Fund (IBTF) Installment Agreement

No cap on the taxes, penalties and interest. Verification of income, expenses, assets and liabilities is not required if the total tax liability is less than $25,000 and paid in full within 5 years. If the total tax liability is more than $25,000 or the tax liability isn't paid in full within 60 months, the IRS will require full financial disclosure.

The IRS will file a tax lien for the total tax liability. And they can force you to sell off business assets. An IRS Revenue Officer WILL visit your business to physically inspect your business's assets. This could be an intimidating experience!

They'll require a corporate officer, shareholder or other responsible party, to determine whether there are any issues with the individual's tax compliance. In other words, the IRS will check that person's history of tax return filing, tax return payments, estimated tax payments, and other tax-related obligations.

IBTF requires the sign off an IRS General Manager.

A pending installment agreement provides protection against IRS levy action, seizure of business assets, and shutdown of the business. If you plan on operating the business for many more years, it's a good idea to enter some kind of installment agreement as soon as possible.

Get three loan denial letters and be ready to produce proof of business asset valuation. That way, you're ready in case IRS asks for this proof.

Current and Compliant

None of the above options is possible unless, and until, the business is current and compliant.

Current involves filing ALL past due payroll tax returns. That's right: file ALL past due payroll tax returns. No matter how many payroll tax returns this amounts to. In many cases, the IRS has filed what's called a Substitute for Return or SFR. However, allowing the SFR to stand in place of an actual and current payroll tax return is a bad idea. See, the IRS estimates the figures of the payroll taxes based on what your business did in the past.

So, if your business experienced a slowdown, the IRS's SFR may be flat-out wrong! It's best to file the proper figures to potentially reduce the total payroll tax liability.

Compliant means that the business begins making payroll tax deposits for the most recent quarter. If the business can't afford to make its payroll tax deposits going forward, the IRS doesn't consider it a viable business. At which point, it's important to face up to the fact that your "baby" has died.

It's not worth putting yourself through anymore aggravation. Just shutter up the business and let much of the payroll tax liability die with the business.

What You Need to be Aware of

If you choose to go it alone by representing yourself before the IRS, know that the IRS Agent WILL attempt to force you into signing form 2750, Waiver Extending Statutory Period for Assessment of Trust Fund Recovery Penalty and form 2751 Proposed Assessment of Trust Fund Recovery Penalty.

I don't recommend you sign either of those documents without first getting tax counsel. See, form 2750 extends the time the IRS can collect on your payroll tax debt. Usually not a good idea to sign anything unless you've been advised appropriately.

Form 2751 may assess you a penalty that's inaccurate because it's based on an SFR (substitute for return). By signing the 2751, you've effectively allowed the IRS to tell you how much you owe them before all the necessary forms are filed to determine the proper amount due.

Not a good idea.

Offers in Compromise

Yes, it's possible for your business to settle your payroll tax debt for less than what you owe. You must be current and compliant. Your business must also produce a completed form 433-B(OIC). Remember, this form lists all business assets, liabilities, and other financial info. It's like filling out a mortgage loan application.

You must provide:

DMV records for business vehicles

UCC filings for business assets, liens, financing

County real estate records for real property

Pacer and other court systems for court records

Credit reports for recent loans and credit applications

Valuation verification using commercial tools (e.g., KBB, Realtor reports, etc.)

For an operating business, expect a visit from the IRS.

Verification of income, expenses, assets and liabilities is not required if the total tax liability is less than $25,000 and paid in full within 5 years. If the total tax liability is more than $25,000 or the tax liability isn't paid in full within 60 months, the IRS will require full financial disclosure.

The IRS is looking for any assets they can find. They want to make sure that you and your business aren't hiding any assets from them! They're basically doing an in-depth investigation of the business.

Collection Appeals Program (CAP)

This refers to a streamlined, fast track appeals process. It requires an IRS general manager follow up within 2 business days.

This type of appeal is usually filed on proposed or actual levy action against the business. It releases the levy due to third party harm and disruption of collection due to a disruption of business operations. Third party harm means that employee paychecks will bounce due to a levy against the business' payroll account.

To get the levy released requires evidence of payroll checks, timecards, etc. The IRS will release the levy up to the amount of payroll checks.

Collection Due Process (CDP) Appeals

Every tax period has the right to only one collection due process appeal. For payroll taxes, this means each quarter qualifies for its own appeal.

Filing CDP only stops enforced collections on the covered tax periods. If there are balances owed for prior years, appeals won't cover those periods.

But it's worth a try to appeal every tax period for which a balance is owed.

It's very rare to avoid personal assessment of trust fund recovery penalties.

The civil penalty can only be assessed against a "responsible" person. The IRS must demonstrate that the responsible person willfully failed to pay over trust fund taxes withheld from employee paychecks. By IRS statute, they're supposed give 60 days to appeal or explore other resolution options. The IRS doesn't also do so because they're in a hurry to get cases closed.

The balanced assessed against the responsible person only includes the principal balance. It does not include penalties and interest assessed against the business.

There are ways to avoid the civil penalty, though. I recommend NOT signing anything unless you get professional advice. No, the guy offering a Groupon for advice doesn't count. Would you really look for the cheapest option when it comes to the life or death of your business? Does your business really matter that little to you? If so, go ahead and let the IRS shut it down.

If you value your business and livelihood, don't, I repeat don't, search out the cheapest option. Doing so could be detrimental to your mental, physical, spiritual and financial well-being. Don't be that guy. You know, the one who's always looking for a deal.

Notice one of the keywords in shortcut is "cut." Don't cut yourself short by seeking the cheapest, safest option. Make sure the tax person has a solid track record of securing results for his/her clients.

Who Must File Form 940?

Most employers pay both a federal (FUTA) and a state unemployment tax. There are three tests used to determine whether you must pay FUTA tax: a general test, household employees test, and farmworkers employees' test.

Under the general test, you're subject to FUTA tax on the wages you pay employees who aren't household or agricultural employees and must file Form 940.pdf, Employer's Annual Federal Unemployment (FUTA) Tax Return, for 2017 if:

You paid wages of $1,500 or more to employees in any calendar quarter during 2016 or 2017, or

You had one or more employees for at least some part of a day in any 20 or more different weeks in 2016 or 20 or more different weeks in 2017. Count all full-time, part-time, and temporary employees. However, if your business is a partnership, don't count its partners.

If you sold or transferred your business during the year, and one of the conditions above applies, you must file Form 940.

However, don't include any wages paid by the predecessor employer on your Form 940 unless you're a successor employer. For details, see "Successor employer" in the Form 940 Instructions. If you won't be liable for filing Form 940 in the future, see "Final: Business closed or stopped paying wages" under Type of Return in the Form 940 Instructions.

For the household employees and farmworkers tests, see Chapter 14 in Publication 15, (Circular E), Employers Tax Guide. Additional information for household employers is available in Publication 926.pdf, Household Employer's Tax Guide and Topic No. 756. Additional information for agricultural employers is available in Publication 51, (Circular A), Agricultural Employer's Tax Guide, and Topic No. 760, Reporting and Deposit Requirements for Agricultural Employers.

FUTA tax rate: The FUTA tax rate is 6.0%. The tax applies to the first $7,000 you paid to each employee as wages during the year. The $7,000 is often referred to as the federal or FUTA wage base. Your state wage base may be different.

Generally, if you paid wages subject to state unemployment tax, you may receive a credit of up to 5.4% when you file your Form 940. If you're entitled to the maximum 5.4% credit, the FUTA tax rate after credit is 0.6%. Generally, you're entitled to the maximum credit if you paid your state unemployment taxes in full on time, and the state isn't determined to be a credit reduction state. See the Instructions for Form 940 to determine the credit.

Credit Reduction State: This is a state that hasn't repaid money it borrowed from the federal government to pay unemployment benefits. The Department of Labor runs the loan program and determines the credit reduction states each year; see FUTA Credit Reduction for more information.

If an employer pays wages that are subject to the unemployment tax laws of a credit reduction state, the credit an employer may receive for state unemployment tax it paid is reduced, resulting in a greater amount of federal unemployment tax due when filing its Form 940 and including the Form 940, Schedule A.pdf, Multi-State Employer and Credit Reduction Information.

You must use Form 940, Schedule A if you paid wages to employees in more than one state or if you paid wages in any state that's subject to credit reduction.

When to File?

The due date for filing the Form 940 is January 31. However, if you deposited all FUTA tax when due, you have until February 10 to file. If the due date for filing a return falls on a Saturday, Sunday, or legal holiday, you may file the return on the next business day. The term legal holiday means any legal holiday in the District of Columbia. For a list of legal holidays, see Chapter 11 in Publication 15, (Circular E), Employer's Tax Guide.

When and How Must You Deposit Your FUTA Tax?

Although Form 940 covers a calendar year, you may have to deposit your FUTA tax before you file your return. If your FUTA tax liability is more than $500 for the calendar year, you must deposit at least one quarterly payment. If your FUTA tax liability is $500 or less in a quarter, carry it forward to the next quarter.

Continue carrying your tax liability forward until your cumulative FUTA tax liability is more than $500. At that point, you must deposit your FUTA tax for the quarter. Deposit your FUTA tax by the last day of the month after the end of the quarter. If your FUTA tax liability for the next quarter is $500 or less, you're not required to deposit your tax again until the cumulative amount is more than $500.

If your total FUTA tax liability for the year is $500 or less, you can either deposit the amount or pay the tax with your Form 940 by January 31. If you're required to make a deposit on a day that's not a business day, the deposit is considered timely if you make it by the close of the next business day.

A business day is any day other than a Saturday, Sunday, or legal holiday. For example, if you're required to make a deposit on a Friday and Friday is a legal holiday, the deposit will be considered timely if you make it by the following Monday (if that Monday is a business day).

Once your FUTA tax liability for a quarter (including any FUTA tax carried forward from an earlier quarter), is more than $500, you must deposit the tax by electronic funds transfer. Generally, you make electronic fund transfers by using the Electronic Federal Tax Payment System (EFTPS). Refer to Publication 966.pdf, Electronic Federal Tax Payment System, A Guide to Getting Started for electronic federal tax payment system information, and Publication 15 for more information on deposit rules.

Incredible **FREE** Gift Offer!

Visit www.SacramentoTaxResolution.com to get your FREE Tax Debt Consultation, a $495 value.

1. From the home page, enter your info where it says, "Do you owe any IRS or state taxes?"

2. Answer the questions.

Voila! Someone from my office will reach out to you!

Steve's business owed $720,000 in payroll taxes; we settled for $7,200.

Chapter 14:

Start with your why.

Start with your why. You've got to have a bigger reason for chasing your goals. Otherwise, when the going gets tough, you'll quickly give up. So, what is your why? What's your motivation for chasing your goals?

Your why must be bigger than just the goal itself. For example, you want to build your business to the million- dollar level. Why? You want to live in a nice house, drive a nice car, and take nice vacations?

All well and good. But your why has got to be bigger than those ambitions. Maybe you have kids. Your why could be that you grew up poor and want to make sure that your kids don't grow up poor. That's better. But what if your why encompassed a much bigger reason? Such as: to start a nonprofit that focuses on teaching kids from underprivileged families how to become entrepreneurs?

And this non-profit would be an offshoot of your business.

You'd feel that motivation whenever you were with a client or put out a marketing campaign. This would be your driving force. No longer would it simply be to have the things you'd always wanted. Although you'd be able to get those things. But getting and having those things wouldn't be your ultimate reason for building your business.

You'd know why before beginning.

See, it's been my experience that the people who quit a lucrative opportunity, without having a fallback plan, are disillusioned due to not beginning with the end in mind. They simply began a career with the hopes of a high income providing lasting satisfaction. As you may know, a high income does not automatically lead to a happy life.

Keeping your why at the forefront of your mind is most important.

If you lose sight of it, you will quickly wander into the sea of forgetfulness. This is when you punch in to work every day, without the end in mind. When was the last time you started driving without a destination in mind? Never?

Don't worry. You're not weird. You're quite normal. If you have started to drive without first deciding on a destination, it's probably because you were either depressed or just wanted to take a drive.

Nothing wrong with either scenario. But, when you hear people rant and rave about the troubles in their lives like, "my boss is just unreasonable. I wish they'd transfer him," or "the bank charged me a fee. They already have plenty of money. Why do we need banks, anyway?" Or some such nonsense. If you asked those people what some possible solutions are, you'd most likely get a deer in headlights look.

That look, is an indication that they just wanted someone to whine to. They don't intend to take steps to improve their situation.

Nope.

Just like the old saying goes, "misery loves company." And it still rings true because most people are merely interested in recruiting "pity partiers."

Never heard of such a thing, you say? That's because it just came to me. Just now.

Since you're looking to improve your lot in life, you are NOT one of those whiners. You're part of the group of elites who are intent on making the world a better place.

Starting with you.

You are both the hardest person to change and the easiest. I read somewhere, "change is hard. But it's also worth it." Change is the one thing you can do without anyone's permission. You can decide right this minute to change. Change is totally up to you. Here's the good news: it's free!

That's right! F-R-E-E. But it ain't cheap.

Change requires new behavior. And if you've ever tried to lose weight, you know exactly what I mean.

Consider challenges.

When you're facing a challenge, you know there are things you can do to overcome them. But, when you know that you're overcoming the challenge because someone else is counting on you to do so, that's just the kick in the pants you need.

The IRS issue you're facing is simply another challenge to overcome. Think about some of the challenges you've already overcome. Let's start way back when you were born. You are,

110

literally, one in a million. You're a fighter. A champion. Out of all the other little sperm, you made it. Then, you were born.

Did you know, according to the CIA, the worldwide infant mortality rate is 5%? So, even though this may not seem like an accomplishment, you lived beyond birth. Then, there's your childhood. You lived and grew up. Another accomplishment. Then you got a job. Then fell in love. Then bought a car. And bought some other stuff.

You've accomplished much.

What's that, I hear? Compared to the Joneses, you haven't accomplished anything? Alas, there's always a temptation to compare yourself with people down the street. But, when I refer to an accomplishment, I don't mean something that someone else has done more of, or bigger than, etc. An accomplishment is something that matters to you.

Don't ever fall into the comparison trap. Because there will ALWAYS be someone to feel inferior to. An accomplishment to you might be as simple as losing 5 pounds. Or paying off $1,000 of debt. Or increased your income by $5,000 per year. It doesn't need to be astronomical. It just needs to be something that took you time and effort to achieve.

But there are also other challenges you've overcome.

You've had situations that no one else knew the solution to. And YOU were the one who came up with the right answer. Whether that was something as small as which movie to watch, which restaurant to go to, or which Netflix show to watch, you've had some wins. The key is not to get caught up in whether the win accomplished huge things.

111

Nope.

If it matters to you, then, frankly, it matters! You're a genius in your own way. Don't get in the way of that. When you do, you rob the world. When you let others miss the joy of your company, insight, or friendship, that's just plain self-centered, don't you think?

Stop the self-sabotage.

What's self-sabotage? Simply put, it's getting in your own way. It's not realizing that you're doing stuff that undermines what you want to do, who you want to be, and where you want to go. You can always tell someone who's committing self-sabotage, because you'll hear them say things like,

"I would take the promotion to manager, but I don't want all the politics."

I want to lose weight, but making my own meals is expensive and I don't have time."

"I would take the classes to get ahead in my career, but they're too expensive."

"I will cheer up, once they apologize."

"I would budget my money, but I don't want to feel restricted."

Those people are committing terrible self-sabotage. So, why do people do this? After all, they claim to want a better result, but simply keep getting in their own way. The quick answer is fear. This little voice in your head that tells you this and that will happen when you step out of the boat, robs so many of success.

Why do people listen to that voice?

Many times, they're afraid of success. Who? what? what? How can someone be afraid of success? Didn't they say they want a better future? It's been my experience; what people say and what people do are two different things.

For example, how many people say they want to lose weight? But you see them eating junk food all the time, not exercising, and using 1,001 excuses for not getting their bloated butts to the gym.

Remember the old saying, "where there's a will, there's a way?" Well, that saying is true. See, when you truly, honest-to-goodness, want something, don't you go after it with every fiber of your being?

For some reason, people are good at pursuing success in their hobbies. But, when it comes down to pursuing the choices that will really make an impact, they suck.

One reason is the outside voices.

Those voices tell them that they're only worthy of a certain result. They believe it. And don't ever strive to climb out of their rut. They choose to embrace the reality others choose for them.

There's one thing you must understand: your life is yours, and nobody else's. You can listen to their advice. You can accept their help. You can even allow them to intervene when you're making wrong choices. But you mustn't allow yourself to get pulled into another person's picture of how your life is supposed to be.

There's another old saying, "Misery loves company." Isn't that a sad reality of life? When we have something to gripe about, we instinctively go out and look for others with the same gripe.

It's almost like we have a sixth sense for those people. Kind of like when you bought a red car and started noticing all the other red cars on the road. Or when you took a vacation to Greece and mysteriously noticed every time someone mentioned "pita," or "Athens."

This is a mystery, indeed.

However, in order to make lasting changes, what you know needs to happen, must meet with the action to make it happen. Otherwise, your dream is only a daydream. These actions, many times, require a degree of change.

Let's face it: change, although helpful for us, doesn't always feel good to us. Change is the one aspect of life we usually resist. I saw a sign in my gym, "You can't expect changes if you don't make any."

Isn't that true?

If something works, don't change it. But, if something isn't working, no matter how long you've done it, change it.

That's not always easy. Why? Because we get used to the way we've always done things.

Our brains are hardwired to develop habits to make life easier. Yet, times change. And, with the changing times, there must be changing habits. When we were kids, mom told us to shower, brush our teeth, and do our chores before heading to school.

That may not be the best advice today. (The chore part, not the showering and brushing teeth part :)) You're employed or have a business, kids, bills, etc. So, waking up and doing the same things, in the same order as when you were a kid, no longer works. So, a different time in your life requires some new habits.

If you've been scatter-brained, either hire someone to help or recruit a friend. In either case, get 'er done. It may not feel good to you, but it may be good for you. Sometimes, doing the hard thing brings the most satisfaction.

Find ways to do what is hardest. Whether you Google it, ask a librarian or ask a friend, find the information and act. After all, "Action beats meditation," every day of the week. Just act.

Even if you don't know all there is to know, act. Even if you're unsure, act. Even if you encounter skeptics, act. No matter what, act.

Just keep moving and good things will happen.

If you hit a dead-end, adjust your direction and keep moving. Pretty soon, you'll develop a wonderful thing called momentum. What is momentum? It's when the things you've been working so hard to see happen, begin happening, with little to no additional effort on your part.

You look like a genius. You look like a superstar. You look like you were born to do this.

There will be blood, sweat and tears on the way. I won't promise you the road will be easy. There will be times when the road will be so miserable, it seems it'd be better to just turn tail and run. The obstacle is too great. The journey is too long. The road is too rough.

That's when it's time to take your cue from college football.

On Sunday, September 3rd, 2017, the incredible happened. Texas A&M went head-to-head with UCLA at the Rose Bowl in Pasadena, California. The two teams appeared evenly matched.

Until the game started.

For the better part of the first three quarters, Texas A&M dominated UCLA in every sense of the word. Rushing, passing, special teams, defense, Texas A&M shut down UCLA. With 4:08 remaining in the third quarter, Texas A&M led UCLA 44 to 10. Talk about domination!

No matter what UCLA tried, it was like Texas A&M had a crystal ball telling them UCLA's next move. It appeared,

the game was over. All hope was lost. UCLA appeared on the verge of ratcheting up the loss.

That's when the tide turned.

First, UCLA drove down the field and scored on a 6-yard run by Soso Jamabo. The commentators, fans, coaches, and everyone else watching, thought this was just a worthless, desperate attempt by UCLA. This made the score 44 to 17, in favor of Texas A&M.

But then UCLA scored again. And again. And again. Now the score was up to 44 to 38. With no timeouts left and facing a fourth down and 6, UCLA's quarterback, Josh Rosen (nicknamed "Chosen Rosen"), drove his team down the field and led UCLA to greatest come-from-behind victory I've ever witnessed.

How did UCLA accomplish this?

Simple. When everyone, including the experts, said the game was over, UCLA didn't. What's the takeaway? The odds are stacked against you, true enough. But that doesn't mean you need to declare yourself the loser. You just need to be a little bit better than your opponent to defeat him.

Don't let the voices from outside deter you. They can be compelling. They can be persuasive. They can also come from someone you love and respect. Don't let them derail you. You won't get anywhere if you do.

They're just voices trying to hold you back from going places. They tell you anything to stop you. Don't listen. The solution is to simply ignore them. Do what mom told you when a bully tried picking on you, "ignore him." It's not always easy, I know.

It appears you're being mean. Or you're lacking compassion. You're giving the bully a piece of his own medicine, without the violence.

Such a move indicates maturity. Yes, you've risen above the temptation of the bully. Yes, he's failed in his attempts to distract you. But he won't quit. Never.

117

He'll keep trying to talk down to you. He'll keep whispering whatever words it takes to get you off course. If you listen to these taunts, you lose. You forfeit the game before you even begin.

What would it look like if you silenced the voices that told you you'd never succeed? What would it look like if you were to win over those critics?

Cue the Braveheart Anthem..." Freedom!" That's what it would feel like. You'd experience that feeling of weightlessness. The feeling that accompanies anything you've ever accomplished.

Remember that feeling? Or has it really been that long since you accomplished anything significant? You know what I mean. The feeling that you get when it seems as though you can do anything. It's as though there are no limits, nothing is impossible.

But it gets lost along the way.

You get bad news. You have a bad day. You get to work late. You lose a major client. Flow lost. And, when the flow gets lost, it's so easy to think it'll never come back. It's easy to think the flow is gone for good.

Is this true? Is the flow really gone? For now, anyway.

The flow isn't entirely gone. It just seems that way. You had it before, you can get it back. Another word for flow is momentum. Momentum is achieved when you do the right things, the right way, for the right amount of time.

You'll know when you've reached momentum because things get easier. You have no explanation why. All you know is good things are happening faster and without much effort on your part. These good things snowball until you make a decision that stops momentum.

Just like it takes effort to gain momentum, it takes effort to keep it going and to get it back. The reason many don't get it back once they've lost it, is because they revel in the days when they used to have it, instead of working to get it back. Let's face it: it's way easier to talk about the past than it is to work towards seeing a better future.

Right?

Especially as we get older. The things we used to have, used to see, used to feel, are what we celebrate. Rather than taking time to put in work to see it happen again, we'd rather gather and talk about how it used to be.

Isn't it tragic to come across people whose best days are behind them? People who lost their drive to excel? Those are the people who were once on the forefront of accomplishing great things but settled along the way.

They allowed themselves to think that what they achieved, was good enough.

No longer do they possess the burning desire to push forward. The obstacles are for the 'other' people to break through. This is a dangerous place to be, especially if you have visions of grandeur. And this may be as simple as saving enough for retirement. Or, seeing your kids get through college. Large or small, this burning desire must keep you pushing forward no matter what.

Otherwise, you risk settling into mediocrity. And nobody celebrates the mediocre anything. Almost isn't good enough. How many Olympic athletes compete for the silver medal? How many people hope they finish second?

Nobody.

You simply can't allow yourself to get caught up on all the things you almost did and achievements you almost gained.

The almost is the enemy of achievement. The old saying "You get an A for effort," only applies when you fail. Think about it. When was the last time someone was told that when they accomplished their goal? The answer is never.

You don't get credit for the things you almost did. Or what you would've done if you had the resources. Or the money.

Don't get caught up in the almost. If you do, you'll almost be successful. If you do, you'll almost achieve a meaningful life. Nothing compares with seeing your dreams become reality. Don't settle for anything less.

What if you faced the giant? What if you won? How would you feel? Who would you tell? There's something magical about imagining your ideal situation. Here's what I mean: when I work out, sometimes I don't feel like pushing myself to do another rep or add weight to the bar. Honestly, doing so is hard.

In order to attain that next rep, I visualize myself struggling to lift the weight. But I always see myself succeeding. It always works. I can't explain it. Yet, seeing myself carrying out the act, with all its grueling details, allows my mind to position itself to see the task through to completion.

What follows is that my body responds positively. Many people are masters at negative visualization. They know how to see what they don't want. But they never take the time to see what they do want.

Ask a dozen people what they want out of life, and they'll tell you all the things they don't want. For some reason, most people don't take the time to think through what they want out of life. Maybe that's why they never get it.

Success is not an accident. Someone said success is a combination of luck, hard work and right knowledge. Earl Nightingale said, "Success is when preparedness meets opportunity."

How many people work hard and know what their favorite celebrity is up to, but don't take the time to learn the right knowledge and stack the odds in their favor?

To achieve goals, you must first set them then work to see them become reality. Without goals, you're aiming at nothing while expecting miracles to happen.

One day, Linus noticed Charlie Brown throwing rocks at the side of a barn. "You're pretty good, Charlie Brown," Linus said.

He said this because he saw that Charlie Brown hit the bull's-eye several times.

"You could say that" Charlie Brown replied. "But you wouldn't think so if you knew that wherever I throw the rock, I just draw the bullseye around it."

If that's you, then we need to make some changes! That's simply no way to work toward your goals. Otherwise, you're praying for the best and getting only the worst.

In order to truly see your goals, become reality, it's important you understand that you need to know what achieving those things will mean to you.

We talked a little bit ago about determining your why. And this is related to it. You must see the goal becoming reality. Imagine yourself driving the car, getting and spending the money, living in the house, marrying your dream person, etc.

If you can't see it, it won't happen. But when you can see through the eyes of faith, it opens doors of possibility.

See, we never fully experience life, until we've seen it in advance.

Picture this: you wake up, without a care in the world. You have plenty of money in the bank. You wake up next to that dream person. You live in your dream house, located in your dream location. All is well with the world.

You give to the causes that interest you. People know your name and are delighted to be known by you.

This is just a taste of what's possible through the power of faith. Now, I don't mean some mystical, hocus-pocus. This is simply visualizing things as you'd like them to be and working backwards from there.

When you know your destination, all you need to do is take the steps to get there. You simply can't go wrong by doing so. Don't you think this beats picturing how you don't want your life to be? What if you tried, just for one week, blocking out anything that doesn't line up with your ideal future.

You refuse to hear, see, talk about, or hear about anything that doesn't help you reach your desired future. This is focus. And when you focus on that outcome, powerful and mind-boggling things happen.

But it takes work.

Yup, you can't sit back on your behind and hope for the best. You've got to see the future and seize it. this is easier said than done, I know. When you decide to work toward a better future, things that you never anticipated going wrong, do. Don't ask me why. They just do. Like Newton's Third Law of Relativity states, "For every action, there is an equal, and opposite reaction."

Catch that.

As soon as you make up your mind to see and seize a better future, it's not going to come easy. And therefore, most people are stuck in their present situation.

They're complaining about not having as good of a life as the next guy. Yet, the time they waste complaining about not having what the next guy has, is time and energy that could've been used working toward a better tomorrow.

Those are NOT the type of people you need to be around.

Those people will, literally, suck the dreams right out of you. Any hope and drive you had will drain right out of your ears. Not really.

But it proves my point.

Surround yourself with people who encourage you to fight and work toward your goals, even if they aren't friends or relatives.

That's right. Sometimes, the people closest to us, discourage us the most. Why? Sometimes, it's because they're jealous. Yes, your brother can be jealous. Yes, your auntie or best friend can be jealous. Many times, jealousy is simply an indication of a resistance to improve. It's fine for you to talk about success. It's fine for you to even attain a little bit of success.

However, as soon as your success begins to snowball, that's when the true colors of your loved ones come to light.

Consider lottery winners. How many of their loved ones don't bother to visit, call or write to them when they're broke.

Yet, once they strike it rich, their third cousin twice removed comes out of the woodwork demanding a piece of the pie.

The guy who mowed their lawn 19 years ago, comes out threatening them with a lawsuit over the $17 that's now turned into $25,000 due to compound interest. Why does this happen?

Well, when people are lazy, they look at the nearest targets. Those people are like leeches: they suck the lifeblood right out of you!

They claim to mean well. They claim that they have your best interests at heart. But, when push comes to shove, guess who they're putting first? That's right, not you!

Those people are dangerous. Be careful. Be wise about who you share your deepest dreams with. If they are insecure about their own future, chances are, they'll do everything in their power to discourage you from pursuing yours.

Another reason people don't support your dreams is because they're afraid. Yes, pure and simple fear. This fear causes them to attack you.

This is the type of person who thinks small. They view you as their competition. You try getting in shape, only to find that it's now a contest between you and your sibling. This thinking causes people to misunderstand that there's plenty to go around.

It also applies to business. When business owners think there's only a limited number of clients to go around, they bite and claw to protect their four and no more. So, when you go knocking on their door offering to do a joint venture, they resist. Their thinking prevents them from experiencing greater results.

It also applies in relationships. When people think there are limited numbers of the opposite sex to go around (fact: there are more than enough women and men to go around) they view you as a competitor once you take steps to improve your chances of finding a quality partner. Don't let yourself get sucked into their mold. Doing so will be the end of you.

Doing so will severely limit the opportunities you pursue. Because "birds of a feather flock together." They're toxic.

Just because they claim to support you, does not mean they will do so.

Am I saying that everyone you know is like this? Not at all.

If you find someone who is genuinely concerned about your wellbeing do everything within your power to keep that person around!

They're golden.

Make sure that it's someone who has weathered some storms with you. Someone who knows that you're not pursuing goals and dreams for selfish motives. Someone who "gets" you.

"We cannot solve our problems with the same thinking we used when we created them." --Albert Einstein

In order to secure a better future, it requires we elevate our thinking. Consider this: when you're frustrated and having your worst day ever, your thinking is NOT on the level of creating plans to improve. Nope. It simply isn't human nature. So, when desiring better circumstances, adjust the way you see your circumstances.

How?

By understanding that most every problem has a solution. Besides natural disasters, political activity, and other situations out of your control, your choices are well within your control.

I heard it said, "We can't control the storm. But we can adjust our sails to weather the storm." it's true. You can't control what other people do, say or think. But you can control how you react.

What's that? You say, "How I react is how I react"? Simply not true. You always have a choice. No matter how challenging the situation, you can choose how you respond, or to not respond at all. You have the power to do so. It simply requires seeing from a different perspective.

This newfound perspective is like a muscle: it must be exercised. It's not developed overnight. It takes time, focus and effort. But it's worth it. When you develop this muscle, situations become just a little bit easier to face.

You may never be perfect with it, but you WILL be better for it. It will elevate you and everyone around you. While I'm not claiming that you can change anyone, I am saying that you can change your approach.

Sometimes, a little bit of honey goes a long way. It sounds like you'd need to kiss up to accomplish this. Maybe. Yet, how's your current approach working for you? Not working? How about this: try a new approach for the next three days. That's right. Just try it out and see if it works for you.

If the new approach gets the same result, go back to your original approach. But, if your new approach gets improved results, stick with the new approach.

While as uncomfortable as attending a new school or your first day on the job, notice how you feel. Maybe you feel accomplished. Or you feel that you reached a higher level in your life. Or maybe you can apply this to your job. Find out if this accomplishes anything worthwhile. Then, after a month or two, teach it to someone else.

If you want to learn a subject, someone said, teach it. It does wonders in deepening the lessons you learned.

Incredible **FREE** Gift Offer!

Visit www.SacramentoTaxResolution.com to get your FREE Tax Debt Consultation, a $495 value.

1. From the home page, enter your info where it says, "Do you owe any IRS or state taxes?"

2. Answer the questions.

Voila! Someone from my office will reach out to you!

Chapter 15:

Roadmap to Resolution

Free Tax Debt Consultation: If you have never been a client of ours, the first step is to call or come in for your confidential, no obligation, free evaluation. At this meeting, an experienced tax resolution professional will evaluate your situation and discuss all available options for resolving your matter.

This generally takes about 30-45 minutes; however, there are times when the information provided at this meeting is not enough to determine a course of action. It is advised that you bring all recent notices and correspondence from the IRS to the meeting.

RETAINING OUR FIRM: At the end of your consultation, and if selected as a good "fit" for our firm, you will be given the opportunity to retain us as your tax representative. You will be required to sign an Engagement Letter and make financial arrangements in order to pay for our tax help services.

We will file a power of attorney (POA) with the IRS. This will provide you with immediate relief because, from this point on, the IRS will be required to contact us instead of you. If they should happen to contact you, all you need to

do is politely request that they contact our firm directly and provide them with our contact information. Also, a separate POA will be required for any State problem you have retained us for.

Beginning the tax resolution process: You will be assigned a case manager who oversees your case. Our case managers are extremely qualified. Our case managers are properly licensed by the federal government to represent you.

Together, we will develop a phased strategy for resolving your case and advise you on what steps to take for the most effective resolution. Your case manager is available to you by phone, email, or in person.

We employ the team approach to resolving your tax problems. Our case managers are supported by a staff of experienced technical specialists who will be your point of contact.

IRS Compliance. Generally, before any negotiation or settlement will be accepted by the IRS, you must become a compliant taxpayer.

Compliance means that all past due delinquent tax returns must be prepared and filed. Compliance also means you must be current on your quarterly estimated tax payments, and you must be withholding at the correct rate, if a wage earner. Your case manager is experienced in what must be done to achieve this and will advise you accordingly. For those of you who can't furnish records necessary to prepare your taxes, we have developed methods, in accordance with IRS regulations, for completing the preparation of tax returns in order to get them filed ASAP.

Your (client) responsibilities: Clients who achieve successful resolution of their matters have the following traits in common: They view the relationship with us as a collaborative one. They view this as a "project" that requires cooperation. They follow through, on a Timely basis, with our requests for information and documentation.

Clients that achieve stated resolution goals return our phone calls, emails and stay in contact with us throughout the duration of their case.

Tax settlement negotiation: We will propose a plan of resolution to the IRS that you can live with and see through to acceptance. We have an excellent IRS settlement track record rate and pride ourselves in obtaining the best (lowest) settlement for you under the law.

However, it is rare that a proposal is accepted right away. Through diligence, persistence and follow-up we will monitor, provide additional information to the IRS as needed, and negotiate your proposed resolution until a resolution is achieved.

Tax resolution is reached: We will review the final resolution of your case by the IRS to make sure it is as agreed upon. If not, we will insist that it be changed to reflect what was agreed to. If the IRS is unwilling to do this, we will advise you as to what your options are for the next step. Finally, you will be advised on what you must do in order to succeed with your resolution and avoid future tax problems.

Sometimes, we work with a client to get to step 6, only to have to start the entire process over again. Why? Is it because we simply forgot about their case? Or, we ignore them? No., it's usually due to the client not responding to our calls and requests for information. Since the IRS can move quickly to aggressively collect taxes owed,

131

I highly recommend quick action on your part. Otherwise, you risk the IRS levying your bank account. This is when they clear out any money you've deposited. When this happens, the money goes into the black hole of your tax bill and is never seen again.

IRS can, and will, also garnish your wages. This involves them notifying your employer that you owe them back taxes so they must deduct it from your paycheck before you ever touch any of it! Were you expecting a tidy bonus? Not so fast! IRS took it!

Believe me, it's in your best interest to take quick action with requests for information. Procrastinating during phase two will leave you hundreds or thousands of dollars poorer.

For some reason, there are people who sabotage their own success. They sense something good is about to happen and don't think they're worth getting it. So, they put off getting the info needed in this phase. Even though the info could be as simple as a signature or two or answering a few questions.

We are working with John, a single dad. He works two nursing jobs because his ex-wife got a judgment issued against him for alimony. So, he works like heck to put food on the table.

John has an IRS issue.

So, he calls us up. He asks our advice. We give it. John signs us up to represent him. John has filed all of his tax returns. He pays our fee. Then, he falls off the planet. We call him, text, email, mail, etc.

But we get no response from him.

We keep on at it...for months...still no response.

As of this date, we still have no idea what happened to John. So, his IRS debt continues to snowball into a bigger and bigger bill. We don't know what will happen to John. All we know is you can learn from him what not to do.

Don't procrastinate!

You've come this far. Why would you throw it all away? Cooperate to see this thing through to the end! After all, if you were trying to lose 50 pounds, would you get discouraged and go back to a diet of Twinkies, hot dogs, soda, and candy bars, just because you only lost 49 pounds?

I didn't think so!

So, why would you get to the finish line of your IRS matter, only to throw it all away? Be not like Nike and just don't do it.

Imagine how your life will look when this gorilla is finally off your back. How will you feel? Where will you go? Who will you tell? What won't you do ever again?

If you're like some of our clients, despite your best intentions, you'll mess it up. Now, we're not saying you will be like our other clients, but there's always a possibility.

Hopefully, you'll buck the trend. Hopefully, you'll step away from the crowd and be an individual. Hopefully.

See, there are some people we've represented before the IRS, who make it all the way to the finish line, only to turn tail and run away from the finish line.

Why?

If you can shed some insight into this mystery let us know. We're still scratching our heads. After all, they've spent thousands of dollars. Spent hours gathering information. And have gone through the trouble of the IRS harassing them. Only to end up right back where they started. Does this make sense to you?

Don't be like those people.

Take Cheri, for example. Cheri was an insurance consultant. Her business was advising insurance brokers in order to help them grow their businesses. During the height of her business, she was doing so well, she overlooked paying her estimated taxes. As a result, IRS filed a federal tax lien against her.

She got one of our introduction letters.

She came in for a consultation. Happy with the advice, she was happy to sign up with us. Then, we didn't hear back from her. So, we waited. And waited. And waited some more. But I'm not one to just a let a juicy prospect wander away. No. So, I did what I do best: send a barrage of emails, texts, letters, faxes, etc. Over the course of about a year, I did everything possible to get Cheri to take action. One day, she e-mailed me saying I should take a break from contacting her.

Now, to be clear, there are two approaches: first, the Stefan approach. This involves being smooth, controlled and downright excellent at attracting the right kind of client.

Second, the Urkel approach. This is where you don't get the client at first, but you keep at it. And keep at it. And keep at it.

That's what I did.

Even though she asked me to ease up, I knew:

1. She had already had her bank accounts levied.

2. IRS threatened to go after other assets and

3. She had an existing federal tax lien, meaning it was only a matter of time before she got a friendly visit from an IRS agent, threatening to throw her into federal prison.

Guess what happened? That's right. One day, I get a panicky call from Cheri. She tells me an IRS agent left her card and a note on her front door warning her that she had a warrant for Cheri's arrest. This meant federal prison time until her time served settled the tax debt. At first, Cheri said she owed IRS around $300,000.

Turned out, with penalties and interest, Cheri owed IRS a whopping $550,000! It was so bad, her case was assigned to the main IRS office in Washington, DC! The agent said that office only handles large cases, including Cheri's.

We settled Cheri's tax debt for a mere $35,000! A savings of over $500,000!

What if you could wave a magic wand and make everything right? How soon would you act? How soon would you wave that magic wand, knowing you could whatever your little heart so pleased? What if I told you, there kind of is a way to make this happen?

Now, I don't mean by waving a magic wand or anything hokey. But what I'm referring to is seeking the guidance of someone who has blazed the path before you. Someone who has helped many others safely pass through to the other side.

And what if you had the opportunity to seek out this person's help with no strings attached? Would you be interested? Well, now you do. You can find out some clues as to how to safely pass to the other side of your IRS issue.

You can find out exactly how to resolve your IRS issue. You don't have to go it alone.

Many people come to me only AFTER they've hit their head against the wall many times. They try handling the IRS issue themselves, only to find out that it's the equivalent of performing your own appendectomy (appendix removal surgery). It's painful. And it's not something you should try at home.

There are surgeons who would gladly perform such a surgery for you. If you needed surgery, would you find that guy advertising on Craigslist, performing surgery out of his garage? Or would you find the most qualified, experienced surgeon?

Right.

So, now you have the chance to work with my firm. We've represented hundreds of clients before the IRS. And have many successful stories to tell. But I prefer not to brag. Take it from Roberto and Lynn: "When we came to them, my wife and I were stressed out because of our IRS issue. We had two nursing homes that were struggling.

We sought their advice on the best way to handle the issue.

They told us it would be best to file all past due tax returns and consult a bankruptcy attorney. We're so glad we followed their advice! Thanks to them, we're getting back on track with IRS.

Anyone who has IRS problems, should definitely go see them!"

You're entitled to a FREE, normally valued at $495, 100% no-obligation, Tax Debt Consultation. During this time, I'll sit down with you, listen to you explain your situation and discuss your options.

Unlike out-of-town firms, you can see us face to face, come down to my office, shake my hand. I mean dozens of your neighbors and co-workers can't be wrong.

I mentioned Steven S. earlier. He works in construction. Here's what he said:

"You guys saved my ass. I'm so grateful I came to you guys. Had it not been for you, I wouldn't be getting married, holding down a good job, and getting my life back together. Thanks so much!"
Randal B. owed the IRS $187,500; settled with them for $1,200!

You can't argue with results.

Incredible FREE Gift Offer!
Visit www.SacramentoTaxResolution.com to get your FREE Tax Debt Consultation, a $495 value.

1. From the home page, enter your info where it says, "Do you owe any IRS or state taxes?"

2. Answer the questions.

Voila! Someone from my office will reach out to you!

CONCLUSION

Would you like similar results? If you answered yes, great! Contact me immediately at **866-859-6420** for your FREE, no pressure, confidential, Tax Debt Consultation. During this meeting, you'll have your options explained to you and you <u>will be heard</u>. There is absolutely no obligation for you to hire me. But, when you do, you'll be so glad you did!

Why? Because I 100% guarantee I will bust my butt to make sure you're well taken care of. You will feel at ease knowing you're represented before the IRS. You won't have to call them, communicate with them, or in any way take time out of your busy schedule to hassle with the IRS.

<u>This normally goes for $495.</u>

Act today and you'll get your very own Tax Debt Consultation...FREE!

So, call 866-859-6420 or email <u>Mike@SacramentoTaxResolution.com</u> right the heck now. Get up and act now! I look forward to working with you soon.

Sincerely,

Mike Ornelas
Enrolled Agent
www.SacramentoTaxResolution.com

"I was extremely skeptical when I first contacted Sacramento Tax Resolution. Mike and his team worked quickly and were able to get the IRS to release two large tax liens that had been looming over me for quite some time. I urge you to contact them!"-**Ryan Petifer**

We won't take your case unless we can help you, GUARANTEED!

We offer the industry leading money-back GUARANTEE: If we don't get you results within 30 days, we'll give you your money back.

Made in the USA
Middletown, DE
11 September 2024

60167785R00077